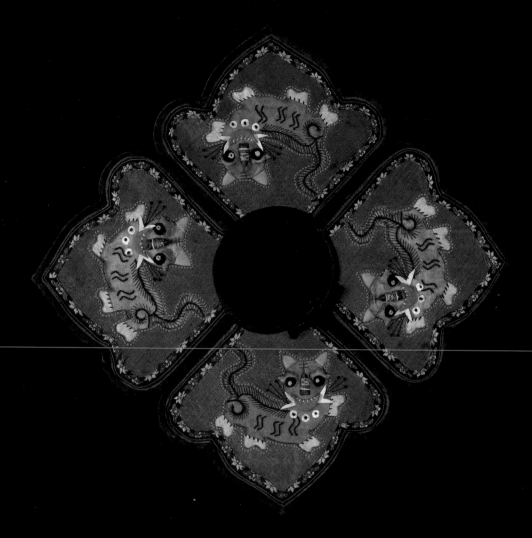

濃 情 滿 襟

Symbolism of Chinese Children's Bibs: A Mother's Affectionate Embrace

胸いっぱいの幸せ

許孩童一個更好的未來！

麗嬰房三十五載，回歸母愛的原點

添一份溫馨與關懷

時間過得真快，轉眼間麗嬰房已經要邁向第三十五年了。雖然公司能夠持續成長，但是每到五年的小階段時，我們總要稍稍停下來回顧、反省與思考以作為前瞻與再出發的依據，最重要的，就是要再度回歸到公司創立的原點：有如媽媽的愛般，為孩子的一切作著想。我們在二十五週年時，出版了第一本書《吉祥童帽》，三十週年的時候又出版第二本書《情繫揹兒帶》，當三十五週年即將到來之際，我們持續努力與耕耘，因此再細心籌畫出版了這部《濃情滿襟》，希望透過孩兒貼身衣物上豐富的刺繡工藝之美，提醒人們莫忘母愛的濃郁與偉大，讓母愛的馨香持續陪伴每一個人，也希望在每一個特殊的週年慶，給企業增添人文的氣息。

回想三十五年前，麗嬰房剛成立時，擔任小兒科醫師的母親給了我單純的靈感與想法：「如何讓小孩子在成長的過程更順利、更健康、更快樂」，我也從創業時就打定了以「孩子是我們一輩子的事業」為麗嬰房的宗旨。三十五年後，這個口號已經成為麗嬰房永續經營的活水源頭，時時提醒我們，要以一個母親對孩兒關愛的心情來經營事業。

基於這些理由，當采如告訴我她想收藏與孩兒有關的民間刺繡與藝術品，並希望可以著手整理與出版時，我就無條件的支持與鼓勵。因為孩子不管是來自富貴家庭，或是貧苦人家，身為父母對小孩的心都是一樣的，以各自的方式表達他們對小孩的「愛」，從童帽、揹兒帶乃至於這些來自各地的圍兜、肚兜和霞帔，都是這個「愛」的表現。能夠把它們收集起來，做有系統的分類，從這些母親們親手縫製的民俗手工藝織品中，去瞭解母愛，我覺得是有意義的工作。

這些一針一線縫製的作品，可能被視為只是常民不足為道的手工藝，可是在「愛」這個價值的座標上，卻是如此豐富和彌足珍貴！

小小刺繡，堅持原創

此外，我們也從前人遺留下來的東西中，瞭解到父母為了要表現他的愛，為了希望他的下一代能夠出人頭地，為了跟別人不一樣，他們所著眼的創新、創意是不得了的。在繁多的收藏品中，我們看到了每一件都是出自母親原創的設計，所收集的繡件幾乎看不到一模一樣的作品，古時候的母親們對創意與設計的高度認真與堅持，也可以給麗嬰房的工作團隊很好的啟示，無論在經營或在童裝和嬰兒用品的設計上，都要堅持發揮創意才能走出自己的路來。

從第一本出版的《吉祥童帽》、《情繫揹兒帶》到這一部《濃情滿襟》，正是我希望能誘發我們工作團隊的創想，也讓承續麗嬰房的人或將來加入麗嬰房的工作伙伴能夠有明確的方向，帶著像母親一般海闊天空的心境，去創造更美好的「愛」的事業。

中、英、日文對照，增添國際視野

「國際化的麗嬰房」，是我們麗嬰房團隊的一個新目標，希望我們企業體能擴及至世界為各地的孩子們服務。也因此，在這部《濃情滿襟》裡，我們刻意將采如的中文本再由采如母女三代翻譯成日文與英文，藉由中、英、日文的對照，呈現母女三代間最真實的情感延續與香火傳承外，也讓這部書得以讓更多不同國籍與文化的人士來閱讀和欣賞。

我也希望我們所有的收藏，包含童帽、揹兒帶、圍兜、肚兜、霞帔、童鞋、童衣等等，在未來能規劃出更理想的展示空間，讓更多人可以近距離品味與欣賞。這其實是一個拋磚引玉的作法，也許將來可以帶動世界各地的人來參與，讓孩子對前人的穿著有所認知，並可以透過這個作法，讓麗嬰房的同仁能有更多元、更廣闊、更國際化的胸襟。

站在麗嬰房三十五週年再出發的起跑點上，我期許麗嬰房展開步伐，為世界的孩子許一個更美好、更廣闊的未來，並願將這一部《濃情滿襟》，獻給普天下偉大的母親。

麗嬰房董事長　　林泰生

Promising a better future for our children!

Time goes by so quickly—suddenly, it seems, Les Enphants is already entering its 35th year. Although the company will always continue to grow, every five years we like to take a moment to think about how far we've come and assess how best to move forward. Most importantly, we like to return to the fundamental mission of this company, which is the desire to serve our clients with the same care as a mother's doting love for her children. For this reason, when we celebrated our 25th year, we published our first book, *Stories of Chinese Children's Hats: Symbolism and Folklore*. At our 30th anniversary, we published our second book, *Bonding via Baby Carriers: The Art and Soul of the Miao and Dong People*. Both books were about mothers who dedicated themselves to making hand-crafted hats and baby carriers for their children. Now that we are upon our 35th year, we want to once again dedicate ourselves to this tradition. Therefore, we have produced this book, *Symbolism of Chinese Children's Bibs: A Mother's Affectionate Embrace*, and hope that through every thread lovingly stitched on these children's bibs, we can all be reminded of the depth and greatness of a mother's love.

Reflecting upon the birth of Les Enphants 35 years ago, I recall my pediatrician mother's simple yet inspirational advice, which she posed in the form of a question: "How do we let a child's growing years be healthier and happier?" It was at that moment that I decided to make our company's motto: "Committed to Children." Thirty-five years later, this motto has become the root of our business, constantly reminding us to care for our company and our clients the very same way a mother cares for her children.

When my wife, Christi, told me she wanted to collect hand-made children's accessories from China, then turn her collections into books, I pledged my support to her unconditionally. All parents, whether from a wealthy family or from a family without means, express their love for their children in whatever way they can. In the case of Christi's collections, parental love is shown through children's hats, baby carriers, and bibs. To collect these tokens of love, to analyze and study them from the perspective of the mothers who painstakingly and lovingly made each piece, is to understand the meaning of love. The pieces of needlework in this book may be ordinary, but in the realm of love, what they express makes them extraordinary.

In these hand-made, hand-woven, and hand-embroidered pieces, a mother's love, hopes, and dreams for her children are expressed through every uniquely creative design. It is love that drives her creativity and therefore, we see that every piece is artistically and emotionally distinct.

This example inspires the Les Enphants family in a profound way—whether it is in managing the business or in designing children's apparel and accessories, we must use love and care in driving our sense of creativity and find a voice all our own.

"Globalization of Les Enphants" is a new direction for our company, one that fulfills the hopes that we can serve children's needs in all corners of the world. For this reason, *Symbolism of Chinese Children's Bibs: A Mother's Affectionate Embrace* is written in Chinese by Christi, translated into Japanese by her mother, and into English by our daughter. This cross-generational and cross-cultural exercise shows the strong ties among these three generations of women, and also allows people from different cultures and backgrounds to enjoy the book.

It is also my hope that Christi's collection, which includes children's hats, baby carriers, baby bibs, baby apparel, and shoes, can one day be showcased together in a more ideal space, allowing more people to appreciate the collection. Maybe one day, children from all over the world can come and view these pieces and learn what Les Enphants is learning: that there is no end to a mother's love, and love can drive creativity to limitless places.

As we stand at the threshold of our 35th anniversary, I deeply hope that Les Enphants will broaden its horizons and create for children everywhere a better and more beautiful future. As well, I hope that *Symbolism of Chinese Children's Bibs: A Mother's Affectionate Embrace* pays proper tribute and homage to mothers everywhere and that all of us, deep in our hearts, are always bound by maternal love forever.

Chairman of Les Enphants co. Eric Tai-sheng Lin

子供たちへ、よりすばらしい未来を

35周年を迎え、「母の愛」という原点に立ち戻る

母の温もりを全ての方々に

時が過ぎるのは実に速いもので、麗嬰房もあっという間に創立35周年を迎えさせていただくことができました。

皆様のお蔭で、弊社は成長を続けているとは言え、これまで5年毎の節目に一旦立ち止まって過去を振り返り、そして反省と思考の上に得た様々なアイディアを、再出発の力の源として参りました。

「いつもわが子を思う母親のような気持ちで仕事に臨む」ということは、会社創立時からの弊社の指針です。初心に立ち戻ることが何より大事だと思っているからです。

そのため、我々は創立25周年に第一冊目の「吉祥童帽」を、30周年に二冊目「情繋揹児帯」を出版しました。

そして来る35周年を迎えさせていただくに際し、私どもは再び真心を込めてこの「濃情満襟」を皆様にお届けさせていただくことに致しました。子供たちの着る服に施した色鮮やかで美しい刺繍工芸を楽しんでいただくとともに、母親の愛情の偉大さを思い出してほしいという我々の願いがこの本に託されています。

またこの本を通じて、これらの作品を作った母親の温かい愛情を多くの人々に感じていただけることも願っています。さらに欲を言うと弊社としては、創立記念というめでたい節目毎に本を出版することにより、職場に少しでも人文的な香りを取り入れられたらと思っております。

振り返れば35年前に麗嬰房が誕生した時、私に一つの助言を与えてくれたのは、当時小児科医師だった母でした。それは「子供たちがより順調かつ健康的に、楽しく成長することをお助けしたい」というシンプルなものでした。そこから、私は創業時から「子供は私どもの生涯のテーマ」を麗嬰房のキャッチフレーズとして参りました。

我々は常に子供を思いやる母親の気持ちで仕事に臨み、そして35年後の今日に至るまで、この言葉は常に弊社の精神のより所であり、いつも我々の気持ちを引き締めてくれています。

そのため、妻、采如が私に子供に関する民間刺繍と芸術品を集め、整理して出版したいと申し出たとき、私は無条件で支持し応援をいたしました。

家庭の貧富の差こそあれ、親から子への愛情には変わりがありません。そして各自のやり方によって子供への愛を、例えば前回の帽子、背負い帯、今回の涎掛け、腹掛け、肩掛けなどを通して表わしていると思います。

母親たちの手で作られた数々の民俗工芸織物を集め分類し、皆様に創作した母親の愛を感じていただくのは、大変やり甲斐のある仕事だと思っています。

これら一針一針手縫いの作品は大した手工芸品ではないかもしれませんが、お金には換えがたい非常に価値のあるものだと思います。

小さな刺繍でも、独創性を堅持する

さらに私たちはこれらの作品により、親から子への愛情、出世して欲しい等の願いを窺い知ることができます。また可愛いわが子のために趣向を凝らした、独特な文様は敬服に値するものがあると思うのです。

数え切れないほどの収蔵品は、どれも強い創作意欲と創意工夫の賜物であり、文様が似通っているものはほとんど見当たらず、弊社のデザイン関連の社員に大変示唆に富む模範を示しています。製作ではベビー服とベビー用品のデザイン、会社の経営においても創意工夫を発揮し、自分のカラーを強く打ち出さなくてはならないことを教わりました。

第一冊目の「吉祥童帽」から、二冊目の「情繋揹児帯」、そして今回の「濃情満襟」の出版は、弊社のスタッフたちへの啓蒙や教育という狙いも込められていると言ってよいでしょう。またこれから弊社を背負っていく者、あるいは入社してくる者にとっても、この本が道しるべとしての役割を果たし、母親の無限に広がる大空のような大らかな心構えで一段と活躍し、より素晴らしい仕事ができるようになってほしいと思うのです。

国際視野を広げるために

世界の舞台で子供達のために活躍できるよう、会社をグローバル化することは麗嬰房が目指している新しい目標であります。そのため、この本は妻が書いた中国語の文章を、さらに義理の母、娘と三人で日本語と英語に翻訳しました。親子三代で協力し合い完成した本ですので、それ自体大変意義深いものであるばかりでなく、より多くの方々に楽しんでいただけることは、なにより嬉しいことです。

私としては、これらの帽子、背負い紐、涎掛け、腹掛け、肩掛け、靴、服、など子供用の小さなコレクションは、より多くの方々が間近で楽しめるように、将来にもっと理想な空間で展示できる事を願っています。

そして、このことを多くの収集家に真似されることも期待しています。そうすれば、より多くの子供が昔の子供たちの身なりや装飾品を理解する機会も増え、また弊社の社員の国際的な視野も広げられるのによりかと思っております。

麗嬰房の35周年の再出発に当り、弊社が時代と共に歩み発展することを願いながら、世界の子供たちのより良き広大な未来を心から祈りこの本を世界中の母親たちに捧げたいと思います。

麗嬰房会長 林泰生

胸前一方小小天地，道盡母親的濃情蜜意

女紅，是含蓄的中國女人傳遞愛的訊息的一種方式，燭光下，伴著夜讀的夫婿做著女紅，它或許是新生兒的一只圍兜，或許是夫婿的一只鞋面，即使是孤燈夜雨，寒意逼人的冬夜，只因屋裡有了這麼一點女紅，一切就變得那樣清潤甜和，溫馨愜意！窗櫺下，女人把絲線細細地劈成幾縷，重重疊疊細密密地，繡成千百種美麗的圖案，女人心中的甜密和對未來的滿心憧憬，就這樣緊緊地鎖在千絲萬縷中，幻化成天地之間生命極致之美！

從很早開始，我就為中國文化中的女紅所深深吸引，夫婿創立麗嬰房之後，以孩子作為我們一輩子的事業，我更為女紅世界中，千萬個女人為孩兒細心縫製的各式用品傾心不已，因為裡面不只是刺繡工藝與藝術之美，更蘊藏了無數母親對孩兒的無私關愛，那才是最讓我感動和低迴不已的珍貴寶藏。

在本書中出現的各式刺繡作品，是我從中國各地陸續探訪蒐集而來的民間工藝品，時間上雖沒有嚴謹的考據，但多數是十九世紀末到二十世紀中後期的孩兒用品，本書歸納分類為《孩兒的第一件衣裳—圍兜》、《兜兜情事—肚兜》、《造型特殊的圍兜》與《美麗的驚嘆號—霞帔》四大項目來介紹這些收藏，而這些繡工細緻的作品，也多半環繞在表現中國人崇尚的吉祥如意精神。希望經過如此的悉心分類與介紹，能帶給人們豐富的精神饗宴！

濃情，從圍兜開始

從孩兒呱呱墜地的那一刻起，母親便把對孩兒的愛，表現在衣食住行的生活瑣事上，圍兜，是許多幼兒的第一件衣服，小小的一塊布，兜在孩兒小小的頸項上，兜起孩兒從今開始的的成長印記，也兜起母親對孩兒綿延細長的深深愛意。

聽說，陝西人稱圍兜為「圍嘴」或「圍圍」（發音yuˋyuˋ），河南人叫 「涎水帕」（「涎」在北方土話發音han ），或叫「口涎」（發音ㄏㄢˊ ㄉㄚ），膠東稱圍嘴為「月亮」，吳語叫「圍饢」，北京俗稱「孩落兒」。

傳統以來，中國的家庭，若是有添丁生兒女的事，無論其家庭的貧富與否，也不管是那個生活階層的人，都視為一件非常令人高興的喜訊，不僅滿月時要備宴或宴客傳達喜訊，而親友亦都準備弄璋弄瓦的禮物回祝道賀，特別是外婆家要為新生兒做成套的衣帽鞋等送去，稱為「頭尾」。其中有些地方的習俗就包含了「圍嘴」這個項目，圍嘴上常常繡有祝福孩兒健康成長、富貴長壽等等帶有吉祥意義的圖案字樣。

當然古時婦女懷孕之時，就待在家裡親自為即將出生的孩兒縫做衣裳，圍兜也是必備之物，因為孩兒一旦開始長牙，勢必流

口水，於是圍嘴就成了不可或缺的實用品，不過一般擦口水的圍兜畢竟和紀念或慶祝出生的圍兜做法不同，目前所收集的圍兜，有些從其做工的講究，以及刺繡的細緻用心看來，應該不是隨擦隨洗的日用品。

關於圍嘴的由來，民間有這樣的傳說：宋朝末年，朝廷腐敗，民不聊生，浙江淳安有一位叫方臘的人物領頭起義，攻州奪縣。官兵和財主見勢不妙，便謠言惑眾，使百姓緊張倉皇之中棄家逃離。一天，義軍經過某村，見全村大人都已逃走，竟只有幾名幼兒躺在搖籃裡。方臘的軍隊悉心餵養他們，走時又燒烤了大薄餅套在孩兒們的頸上。眾百姓回家，見到小孩兒安然無恙，非但沒有餓死，反而更加健壯，便非常地高興。方臘起義失敗後，婦女們為感念方臘的義行，便仿照大薄餅，悉心繡製了圍嘴，此後，從大薄餅演變而來的圍嘴，便漸漸成為幼兒成長過程中，頸項胸前最貼心的守護神。

直到現在，台灣民間仍保存著一個習俗，在孩兒四個月大時，母親會將類似大薄餅的圓餅，以絲線圈住綁在孩兒的脖子上，叫做「收涎」，希望孩子不再流口水，不知是否和宋朝方臘的民間習俗有關。

肚兜，傳說中女媧賜予凡人的第一件衣裳

至於肚兜，則是貼掛於胸腹的一種裝飾。根據民間的傳說，肚兜的起源可以追溯到女媧氏時代，傳說肚兜是女媧造人之後留給後代的第一件衣服，當然它的實用性在於蔽體，而且我們從小就聽長輩說：「小心肚子著涼了。」所以肚兜也是為了保護肚子而穿的。肚兜的形狀像背心的前襟，大多呈菱形，上面以帶子繫在脖子上，下面兩邊的帶子就繫在腰間，古時候天熱的時候，常可看到小朋友只穿了一件肚兜在院子玩耍的場景。

肚兜的圖案也和吉祥如意有關，例如繡上八卦的圖案，有天時，地利，人和的含意；若是繡上虎頭像，則有虎虎生風，威風凜凜的意思；有的祈求孩子前途遠大考試高中；有的希望蓮生貴子（連生貴子），家中人丁興旺。

和圍兜一樣，婦女有喜後，母親和婆家也都要為快出生的娃娃縫製肚兜，有些地方的習俗是端午節時，舅舅要給小外甥送肚兜，上面繡有五毒，指五月時分百蟲復甦，瘟病易起，繡上五毒有驅病害保健康的美意。

其實不僅小朋友穿肚兜，有時未過門的媳婦要為將來的丈夫縫肚兜，將來新婚夫婦穿肚兜上面繡了象徵夫妻恩愛的圖案。壯年人到了「過門坎兒」的年歲，也會換上新肚兜兒圖

個平安。老年人到了「過門坎兒」的忘年，就由閨女為老人家做肚兜以求長壽。因此肚兜除了實用之外，也充分體現民俗文化的特質。

有些肚兜，雖然上面帶有吉祥意味甚至與男女愛情相關的圖案，分不太出來是給小孩抑或成年人穿戴的，若以尺寸來區分，則大致可以區隔出來。收集在本書的肚兜，尺寸便以在寬度48公分以下，長度42公分以下的為主，以別於成人穿戴的肚兜。

豔麗似彩霞的霞帔

「雲肩」其實在古代是重要服飾之一。隋代的觀音像即有披雲肩者，在敦煌唐代壁畫中亦見到貴族婦女使用雲肩，因此可知穿著雲肩的習俗應不會晚於隨唐。另有一說，指早在秦漢時期已有雲肩，那時用細絹製作的一種長條圍巾式的披帛，以及魏晉南北朝時期的繡領。隋唐時期人們讚美這種服飾豔麗似彩霞，故又稱為「霞帔」。

到了元代，雲肩更是普及了，而且男女皆穿用，貴族男女通行穿著「四合如意式」大雲肩，並定位官服式樣，明代洪武年曾有規定：一、二品命婦霞帔，用蹙金繡雲霞翟紋；三、四品命婦霞帔，用金繡雲霞孔雀紋。到了清末，雲肩更加流行，成為禮服的一部份，民間婦女在婚慶或重大節日時才穿戴。

基本上，雲肩分「四合如意式」和「柳葉式」兩種，但從中又衍生出各種樣式來。本書介紹了幾件小兒類似雲肩的衣飾，以其頸圍之大小因而推定可能為小兒所用。

本書得以順利付梓，我要特別感謝陝西西安美術學院的王寧宇老師、山東煙台師院學院的山曼老師，以及黏碧華老師的協助與指正。感謝我的母親藍劉玉嬌女士及女兒柏薇的日、英文翻譯，以及劉美玉、林惠玫、蘇曉晶、朝台鳴、謝家蘭、賴芳英、小熊千晶等諸多朋友的協助。

英文部分有賴印第安那波里斯大學出版社編輯David Hanna及Lauren Cregor之細心校正，同時該校出版社社長藍朵風教授長期予「吉祥童帽」、「情繫背兒帶」以及本書持續不斷於歐美博物館及圖書中心推廣介紹。謹此致謝。最後，我的夫婿林泰生對我收藏的熱誠始終是最忠誠的鼓勵者與支持者，深深銘感於心。

不管是圍兜、肚兜，或是霞帔，幼兒小小的胸前，承載的是女人滿滿的柔情，與身為母親的無私祝福。濃情滿襟，又豈能不加以細細體會！

麗嬰房顧問董事　藍朵如

Preface and Acknowledgements

Needlework is the way that modest Chinese women expressed their love. Under the warm glow of candlelight, she might be sewing a bib for her newborn baby, or may be embroidering shoes for her husband. It could be a windy, rainy night, or in the dead of winter, but the image of a woman with her needlework immediately warms the heart. Beneath the window, she spins thin thread upon thin thread, the multitude of colors overlapping and criss-crossing each other, tightly bound together, magically producing extraordinary designs.

I have always been deeply fascinated by the Chinese culture of needlework. After my husband started Les Enphants and "committed [us] to children," I found myself in the thick of the world of needlework. Millions of women sew and mend all kinds of apparel and accessories for their children, but it is not merely the sheer beauty of this art that fascinates me, it is the love that is threaded into every stitch that truly moves me.

The items collected in this book come from the various places I have traveled in China in recent years. Though I do not have the exact age of every piece, most of the children's apparel and accessories I have collected are dated roughly from the end of the 19th century to the middle of the 20th century. This book is separated into three main sections: the bib *(wei zwei)*; the undergarment *(du dou)*; and the capelet *(yun-jian or xia-pei)*.

Wei Zwei—The Bib

From the moment a child is born, the mother will express her love for this child through all the seemingly mundane everyday objects that the child needs and uses. The bib is often the very first piece of accessory the baby uses. This tiny piece of fabric, secured around the child's little neck, ties together the child's first memories with his mother's unending love.

According to Chinese tradition, a child's birth is always celebrated with the greatest elation. When the baby is one month old, family and friends celebrate at banquets and gifts are showered upon the baby. The mother's side of the family, especially, is responsible for preparing a complete set of clothing for the baby—clothing and accessories that will cover the baby from head to toe. Included in this list is the bib, upon which there are often embroidered sayings and symbols wishing the newborn a long and successful life.

Of course, in the old days, when women were pregnant, they would stay at home and make every piece of clothing for their babies by hand. The bib was always a must, because as soon as the baby started teething, he would inevitably drool a lot. Therefore, the bib became an indispensable item. However, it is clear that the bibs for everyday use and the ones used for celebratory purposes (as in the baby's one-month banquet) are quite different in design and intricacy.

According to folklore, the bib came about in this way: At the end of the Song Dynasty, during a time of great uncertainty, a man named Fang La from Zhejiang Province led an uprising against the corrupt government. The government and landlords spread rumors against Fang La, which stirred up even greater unrest, and citizens began abandoning their homes to find safety in remote places. One day, as Fang La's army passed through a small village, they saw that the whole village had run away, leaving behind their babies, who were crying in their cribs. Fang La's army fed and cared for the babies, and before departure, they tied large, round flatbreads around the babies' necks, so the babies would not die of hunger. When the villagers returned and saw that not only had their babies survived, they had all grown bigger and looked healthier, they were surprised and very happy. After Fang La's righteous revolution was defeated, the women from this village wanted to commemorate Fang La's good deed, so they began embroidering pieces of fabric to mimic the large round flatbreads that the army had tied around their babies' necks. Thus, the bib was born, and this small piece of fabric that covers babies' chests became a symbol of protection.

Today in Taiwan, there is this tradition: When a child is four months old, the mother will string round cookies onto a thread and tie it around her child's neck. This tradition is perhaps tied to the Song Dynasty folktale about Fang La.

Du Dou—The Undergarment

The undergarment is a piece of clothing that covers the chest and abdomen. According to folklore, the invention of the undergarment goes back to the times of Nü Wa. It is believed that after creating mankind, the undergarment was the first piece of clothing that Nü Wa left for mankind. Of course, the undergarment has its practical attributes. As youngsters, we would often hear adults tell us to take care not to "let our stomachs catch a cold," since the Chinese believe that even a gust of wind passing through one's belly button could make a child sick. So the undergarment was traditionally worn to keep the belly protected. The undergarment is a piece of argyle-shaped cloth that covers the chest and belly, while the back is left open. The top is tied around the neck, and there are strings on either side of the waist that are tied behind the back. Back then, when it was hot, children could often be seen wearing just an undergarment. Think of the undergarment as a backless undershirt.

 The designs and symbols on the undergarment have to do with fortune and good luck. For example, the symbol of the Eight Diagrams represents the elements (both celestial and earthly) such as heaven, fire, thunder, wind, and water. Each of these elements represents a quality— for example, heaven is power and water is complacency. Or, if the

undergarment has an embroidered tiger's head on it, the mother is trying to protect her child from harm and she hopes that the child will grow up to be successful in serving in the court and in society.

As with the bib, when a woman finds out she is with child, her mother and mother-in-law will quickly take to making undergarments for the soon-to-be-born child. In some places, the tradition is that, during the Dragon Boat Festival, it is the responsibility of the uncle (the mother's brother) to present his niece or nephew with an undergarment with the Five Poisons (the viper, scorpion, centipede, toad, and the spider) embroidered on it. Together, these have the power to protect against illness. Therefore, this particular gift is meant to wish the young child good health.

In fact, it is not only young children who wear undergarments. It was tradition for a young woman about to be wed to sew an undergarment for her soon-to-be husband. After the couple is married, they will both don undergarments with symbols on the front that represent a happily married couple. When older people approach the end of the decade age—for example, when they are 69, about to turn 70, or 79, about to turn 80—it would have been the responsibility of an unmarried girl to make an undergarment for them to pray that they safely leap toward a new decade of age. The undergarment has practical uses, but it is also itself a symbol of culture and tradition.

It is sometimes difficult to tell, even with undergarments that depict love stories between men and women, whether they are meant for children or adults. But if we use measurements as a way of differentiating, we would probably know more or less which undergarment belongs to whom. The *du dou* undergarments collected in this book are less than 48 centimeters in width and less than 42 centimeters in length, which are sizes more likely made for children.

Yun Jian or Xia Pei—The Capelet

The capelet was a very important piece of clothing in the olden days. Paintings and idols of Guan Yin (Goddess of Mercy) from the Sui Dynasty (6th-7th centuries) always depict her wearing a capelet. In Tang Dynasty (618-907) murals in Dun Huang caves, women of the higher classes are also depicted wearing capelets. Thus, it can be inferred that the use of capelets began no later than the Sui (581-618) and Tang Dynasties. There is also reason to believe that capelets were even worn in the Qin-Han era (2 B.C. – 2 A.D.). During the Jin (265-420) and Southern-Northern Dynasties (420-581), elaborately embroidered collars were worn. Capelets were called *yun jian*, or "cloud shoulder," because their beauty and variations reminded people of moving clouds.

By the Yuan Dynasty (1271-1368), it was common for both men and women to wear capelets. Men and women from the upper class would wear larger capes. Capelets with four *ru-yi* divisions were the symbol of someone working as a government official. In the Ming Dynasty (1368-1644), wives of the first- and second-rank officers were allowed to use gold thread of the best quality to embroider cloud motifs and mountain pheasants on their capelets. For the third- and fourth-rank wives, gold thread of the next grade was used to embroider clouds and peacocks on their capelets. By the end of the Qing Dynasty (1644-1911), capelets were very much in vogue, and women of all classes would wear them for weddings and other special occasions.

In general, there are two types of capelets: the four-part *ru-yi* style and the willow leaves style. In this book, we introduce a few that are children's capelets, which we have determined to be such by the circumference of the neck.

For centuries, whether in bibs, undergarments, or capelets, mothers have expressed their boundless love for their children. In every stitch and every thread on those small pieces of fabric, a mother's hopes and dreams are sewn. Indeed, tied around her child's neck, it is the ultimate symbol of a mother's embrace!

Acknowledgements

For the swift completion of this book, I have to thank Professor Ning-yu Wang, Professor Shan Man, and Professor Bi-Hua Nian for their generous help and patient direction. I would like to thank my mother, Dr. Yu-chiao Liu Lan, and my daughter brenda Lin for their Japanese and English translations. As well, I would like to thank Pamela Liu, Huei-mei Lin, Ivy Su, Fang Ing Lai, Chiyaki Oguma, Tai-Ming Chao, Marina Hsieh and all the friends who have supported this modest endeavor. My thanks also go to the editorial staff, David Hanna and Lauren Cregor, of the University of Indianapolis Press for their editing of the English edition. I am especially grateful to Dr. Phylis Lan Lin, Executive Director of the University of Indianapolis Press. Dr. Lin has been a steady source of support in introducing symbolism in Chinese folk arts to the west via my collections illustrated in my three books: *Stories of Chinese Children's Hats: Symbolism and Folklore, Bonding via Baby Carriers: The Art & Soul of the Maio & Dong People,* and *Symbolism of Chinese Children's Bibs: A Mother's Affectionate Embrace*. Last, but certainly not least, I would like to thank my husband, Eric Lin, for his unconditional support in my passion for collecting these items and in helping me translate these collections into books.

Les Enphants co. Consulting Director   Christi Tsai-ru Lan Lin

【 まえがき 】

大きな愛情からなる小さな涎掛け

女の針仕事は教養ある中国の女性が愛のメッセージを伝える方法の一つと言えるでしょう。明かりの下で読書をする夫の側での針仕事、それがやがて新生児の一枚の涎掛け、あるいは夫の靴の表面の飾りになったりします。寒さ迫る冬の夜でのその光景は甘く、心暖まる雰囲気の下で将来への憧れを一針一針縫い込み、千差万別の美しい図案を作り出したのでしょう。

大分以前から私は中国文化の中でも、針仕事には深く惹きつけられてきました。主人が麗嬰房を創立してからは、子供たちは我々の生涯のテーマとなり、そして益々私は子供のために作られた様々な細かい母の針仕事に心を奪われるようになりました。それは刺繍工芸と芸術の美としてだけではなく、その中に隠されている母親からわが子への無償の愛が、私に深い感動をもたらしたからです。

この本の中に出てくる各種の刺繍作品は、私が中国各地で探し収集した民間工芸品です。しっかりした時代的な裏づけはありませんが、大体19世紀の後期から20世紀の中期頃の子供用品です。この本を四大項目に分け、これらの収蔵品を紹介していきたいと思います。細やかな刺繍作品にはめでたい図案が多く、中国人がいかに縁起を担ぐことが好きなのかを物語っています。この本が、私たちのより豊かな精神の糧になることを切に願っています。

涎掛けに始まる愛情

赤ちゃんが産声を上げると、母親の愛情は生活のこまごまとした面に表現されていきます。涎掛けは多くの赤ん坊が最初に身につける衣服の一つで、赤ちゃんの首に掛けられる胸の小さな一枚一枚の布は、その成長の印でもあり母親から赤ん坊への末永く深い愛情の表れでもあります。

聞くところでは、中国の陝西の人は涎掛けのことを「圍嘴」あるいは「圍圍」、河南の人は「涎水帕」あるいは「口涎」、山東の人は「月亮」、呉語では「囲食」、北京語では「孩落兒」とそれぞれ呼んでいます。

昔から中国では赤ん坊が生まれるのはその家の貧富に関わらず人生の一大喜びでありました。そして満一ケ月（満月）には喜びを親戚、友人と分かち合うために、宴席の招待やお祝いのために用意したお赤飯などを配ります。 また、親戚、友人も贈り物をします。特に産婦の里方は赤ちゃんのための帽子から靴にいたる一式の衣服類を娘の所に届けます、これは「頭尾」という習慣です。地方によっては涎掛けがその中に入っていることがあります。それにはいつも赤ちゃんの健康と成長を祝福し、裕福と長生きの意味が込められている文様が入っています。

昔の女性は妊娠すると、自ら赤ちゃんの衣服を縫い始めます。赤ちゃんは歯が生え始めると必ず涎を流しますので、涎掛けは欠かせないものですけれども、日常用のものと記念的な意味を持つ涎掛けの作り方はまったく違っていて、現在コレクションしている涎掛けはその作り方や刺繍の細やかさから見れば、大変上等なものであり、日常的に使われるようなものではなく記念的なものであることが分かります。

涎掛けの由来を辿れば、民間ではこのような言い伝えがあります。約千年前の宋の時代の晩期、朝廷は腐敗しきっており、方臘という人物が一揆を起こしたため、国は混乱に陥り人々は逃げ回っていました。そんなあるとき、とある村に通りかかった一揆軍は大人たちに置き去りにされた何人かの幼児を見つけました。不憫に思った一揆軍は飢え死にしないように大きな丸い煎餅を焼き、糸を通して子供たちの首に掛け、お腹が空いたらいつでも食べられるようにして去っていきました。後に村人が戻って来たとき子供たちの無事を確かめ大いに喜び合い一揆軍に感謝しました。

方臘の蜂起は失敗に終わりましたが、彼らの心ある行いを感謝し、人々は煎餅の形に似た涎掛けを作り記念にしました。それ以来、丸い煎餅が元になったといわれる涎掛けは子供たちを優しく守るようになったのです。

今でも台湾では赤ちゃんが満4ケ月になると、丸い煎餅のようなお菓子に糸を通して赤ちゃんの首に掛け、「収涎」といって子供の涎を止める風習があるのは、やはり方臘の話と関係があるかも知れません。

腹掛け、伝説の中女媧と言う神様が人間に与えた最初の衣装でもあり

腹掛けは伝説中の女神、女媧さまが人間に与えた最初の衣装と伝えられています。腹掛けは胸と腹を覆う一枚の布です。伝説によると女媧さまが人間を作ったとき人間に与えた最初の一枚の衣装で、体の一部を覆う実用性のあるものでした。私たちは幼少の頃から、「お腹を冷やすな」と親からよく注意されたものです。腹掛けはまさにお腹を守るために付けるもので、菱形をしていて襟元に二本、腰の両サイド二本、それぞれに紐があり、首の後ろと背中に紐を持って来て結びます。背中はほとんど何も着ていない状態になります。中国の古い絵画では、夏場にこの格好をして庭で戯れる子供たちがよく登場します。

腹掛けの文様もまた縁起物がとても多く、例えば八卦の文様には、頃合がよく．場所が有利．人と上手くやっていけるというめでたい意味が込められています。また虎の文様は虎の威風堂々としている様を示し、さらに子供の出世．試験合格願い、蓮の花の文様なら子孫繁栄を願うものです。

また、妊娠すると涎掛けと同じように、姑と里方では生まれる赤ちゃんのために腹掛けを作り始めます。端午の節句の頃には色々な虫の活動が活発になり、流行病をもたらし易いので、地方によっては里方の男の兄弟が生まれる甥の為に五つの毒「五毒」の文様を施した涎掛けを贈ります。病気を退治し、健康が保てますようにという優しい心使いです。

実際には子供だけが腹掛けを使うわけではなく、婚約して結婚を控えているお嫁さんは、将来の夫と自分のために腹掛けを作る習慣もあります。その場合夫婦円満の意味を持つ文様を施します。また壮年になると、年齢の節目に腹掛けを作り、無事を祈る習慣もあります。娘がある年齢に達した親のために腹掛けを作り長寿を願うこともあります。従って腹掛けには実用性のほかに、民間の様々な習俗も十分反映しています。

また、一部の腹掛けには縁起物や男女の愛情に関するような文様が施され、子供用なのか大人用なのかの区別が付かないものもあります。この本に収録されている腹掛けは幅47センチ以下、丈42センチ以下のものが多く、主に子供用のものです。

艶麗の如き霞の様な色彩―霞披

「雲肩」とも呼ばれる肩掛けは、昔では重要な飾りの一つです。6世紀から7世紀にかける隋の時代では、観音様の像にも肩掛けが見られ、敦煌にある7世紀初頭から始まる唐の時代の壁画からも、上流社会の女性が肩掛けを使っていたことが判ります。遅くとも隋か唐の時代には肩掛けが着用されていたことが伺えます。また一説によりますと、2千年前の秦と漢の時代にすでに細緻な絹で作った長いスカーフのような肩掛けがあったようで、またその直後の魏晋南北朝の時代にも刺繍した襟巻きが用いられていたようです。隋と唐の時代には人々はそれらの霞のように美しい色合いに魅了され、「霞披」と呼ぶようになりました。

14世紀から始まる元の時代になると、肩掛けは一般的になり、男性まで着用するようになりました。貴族男女の間では「四合如意様式」の大きめの肩掛けが流行り、官服として着用の規則まで決められていました。明の時代の初期の洪武皇帝の時代になると、地位のもっとも高い一品、二品高官の夫人方は上等の金糸刺繍であしらった雲翟文の肩掛けを、そして次の位の三品と四品の貴婦人方は金糸で孔雀文の刺繍と決めた程になりました。最後の王朝清の時代になると、肩掛けはさらに広く流行し礼服の一部にもなり、民間の女性も結婚やその他の重要な冠婚やお祝いの行事で身に付けるようになりました。

基本的には肩掛けは「四合如意様式」と「柳葉様式」の二つに分けられます。しかしそれらからまた色んな様式が生まれました。本書は首周りのサイズから子供用と思われる肩掛けも何点か取り上げました。

本書が出版することができましたのは、一重に皆様のお陰です。特に陝西西安美術学院の王寧宇先生、山東煙台師院学院の山曼先生、並びに粘碧華先生のご指導とご協力に、心から感謝申し上げます。更に私の母、藍劉玉嬌女史、娘の柏薇には日本語訳と英語訳を担当してもらい、劉美玉、林恵玫、蘇暁晶、朝台鳴さん、謝家蘭さん、頼芳英さん、小熊千晶さんを始めとした多数の友人たちにもご協力を頂き、大変嬉しく思っております。ありがとうございました。

英語の部分はIndianapolis大学出版社編集、David Hanna及びLauren Cregorの心使いの校正によったものです。又、この大学の出版社社長藍采風教授は長期にわたり、「吉祥童帽」「情繋背児帯」及び本書への絶みないご協力や本の世界市場への推選等の頑張りに対しここに深く感謝の意を表します。最後に私の主人林泰生は私の収蔵に対して終始最も熱誠で大いに励みと後援をいただき、感謝の気持ちで胸が一杯です。

涎掛けばかりでなく、腹掛けも、肩掛けも、女性の優しい心使いと母の暖かい祝福が込められています。まさに胸いっぱいの幸せです。是非ご堪能ください。

麗嬰房顧問董事　藍采如

目　錄

出版緣起　**許孩童一個更好的未來！**麗嬰房三十五載，回歸母愛的原點 ……………… 林泰生 **2**

前言　　　**胸前一方小小天地，道盡母親的濃情蜜意** …………………………… 藍采如 **5**

第1部　幼兒的第一件衣裳---圍兜

第壹章　山林氛氳　　　　　　　　**16**
龍紋 ……………………………………… 16
獅紋 ……………………………………… 21
虎紋 ……………………………………… 23
太平有象 ………………………………… 27
豬形圍兜 ………………………………… 29

第貳章　水波蕩漾　　　　　　　　**30**
魚紋 ……………………………………… 30
蟾蛙坐蓮 ………………………………… 32
科舉高中 ………………………………… 33

第參章　蝶亂蜂喧　　　　　　　　**34**
功名富貴 ………………………………… 34
花中之舞 ………………………………… 36
小動物 …………………………………… 39

第肆章　落英繽紛　　　　　　　　**41**
花中之后 ………………………………… 41
冰霜鐵骨 ………………………………… 42
四季平安 ………………………………… 43
百花齊放 ………………………………… 44
瓜瓞綿延 ………………………………… 45
葫蘆 ……………………………………… 47
連中三元 ………………………………… 48

第伍章　民間故事與神話　　　　　**49**
西遊記 …………………………………… 49
龍生,虎奶,雕打棚 ……………………… 50
武松打虎 ………………………………… 51
苗族神話 ………………………………… 52
暗八仙/暗八寶 ………………………… 54

第陸章　童玩世界　　　　　　　　**55**
嬰戲圖之一─童子玩爆竹 ……………… 55
嬰戲圖之二─吹簫玩扇 ………………… 57
嬰戲圖之三─童子執蓮花 ……………… 58
嬰戲圖之四─福壽無疆 ………………… 59

第柒章　綿延的祝福　　　　　　　**60**
吉慶連續紋 ……………………………… 60
八卦 ……………………………………… 62
哪吒 ……………………………………… 63
如意雲紋 ………………………………… 64
回紋 ……………………………………… 66
銅錢紋 …………………………………… 67
長命鎖 …………………………………… 69

燈籠紋 …………………………………… 71
人紋 ……………………………………… 72
吉祥字 …………………………………… 73
抽象的圖案 ……………………………… 75

第2部　兜兜情事---肚兜

第壹章　絲竹之美　　　　　　　　**78**
《拾玉鐲》 ……………………………… 78
《天仙配》 ……………………………… 80
《桑園會》 ……………………………… 81
《麥仁罐》 ……………………………… 82

第貳章　民間故事與神話　　　　　**83**
劉海戲蟾 ………………………………… 83
太極 ……………………………………… 84
麻姑獻壽 ………………………………… 85

第參章　文人雅風　　　　　　　　**86**
琴棋書畫 ………………………………… 86
竹 ………………………………………… 88

第肆章　愛的喜悅　　　　　　　　**89**
鴛鴦戲水 ………………………………… 89
鳳戲牡丹 ………………………………… 90
多子多孫 ………………………………… 91
麒麟送子 ………………………………… 92
天仙送子 ………………………………… 93
洞房花燭夜 ……………………………… 94

第伍章　花團錦簇　　　　　　　　**95**
花團錦簇之一 …………………………… 95
花團錦簇之二 …………………………… 96

第陸章　吉獸報喜　　　　　　　　**97**
青獅 ……………………………………… 97
獅子戲球 ………………………………… 99
鶴 ………………………………………… 100

第柒章　望子成龍　　　　　　　　**101**
指日高陞 ………………………………… 101

第捌章　祛毒避邪　　　　　　　　**102**
五毒 ……………………………………… 102

第玖章　成人肚兜　　　　　　　　**104**
客家肚兜 ………………………………… 104
春耕圖 …………………………………… 105
梅花鹿 …………………………………… 106
蓮 ………………………………………… 107

第3部　造型特殊的圍兜

第壹章　爭奇鬥豔　　　　　　　　**110**
有鳳來儀 ………………………………… 110
桃形圍兜 ………………………………… 112
蝶形圍兜 ………………………………… 113
果形圍兜 ………………………………… 114

第貳章　裝飾性強的圍兜　　　　　**115**
美麗的流蘇之一 ………………………… 115
美麗的流蘇之二 ………………………… 117
美麗的流蘇之三 ………………………… 118
華美的圍兜之一 ………………………… 119
華美的圍兜之二 ………………………… 120
華美的圍兜之三 ………………………… 121
華美的圍兜之四 ………………………… 122

第參章　方形的圍兜　　　　　　　**123**
方形的趣味之一 ………………………… 123
方形的趣味之二 ………………………… 124

第肆章　有趣的圍兜　　　　　　　**125**
背心式的圍兜之一 ……………………… 125
背心式的圍兜之二 ……………………… 126
特殊的圍兜之一 ………………………… 127
特殊的圍兜之二 ………………………… 128
特殊的圍兜之三 ………………………… 129

第4部　美麗的驚嘆號---霞帔

第壹章　造型之美　　　　　　　　**132**
柳葉霞帔 ………………………………… 132
蝶形霞帔 ………………………………… 134
桃形霞帔 ………………………………… 135
霞帔之美之一 …………………………… 136
霞帔之美之二 …………………………… 137
霞帔之美之三 …………………………… 138
成人霞帔之一 …………………………… 139
成人霞帔之二 …………………………… 140
成人霞帔之三 …………………………… 141

參考書目 ………………………………… 142
作者‧譯者簡介 ………………………… 143

Contents

Froward .... Eric Tai-sheng Lin **3**

Preface and Acknowledgements .... Christi Tsai-ru Lan Lin **6**

Part I *Wei Zwei* – **The Bib**

Chapter 1   Powerful Animals **16**
The Supreme Force—The Dragon 16
Symbol of Intelligence—The Lion 21
Lively and Vigorous—The Tiger 24
Signs of Peace—The Elephant, The Deer, and The Ox — 27
Contentment Brings Happiness—The Pig 29

Chapter 2   Auspicious Aquatic Animals **30**
Surplus and Abundance Every Year—The Fish 31
Wa Wa—The Frog 32
Crab 33

Chapter 3   Busybees– Birds and Insects **34**
Laurel Achievement and Rich Life—The Bird 35
Dancing Among Flowers—The Butterfly 37
Small Animals—Birds and Beasts 39

Chapter 4   Flowers and Plants **41**
Queen of Flowers—The Peony 41
Plum Blossom 42
Peace for All Seasons—The Four Seasons 43
All Flowers Are In Bloom 44
To Have Many Descendants—Melons 46
Hu-Lu—The Gourd 47
The Three Accomplishments 48

Chapter 5   Folk Tales and Fairytales **49**
Journey to the West 49
A Hero Raised by Nature 50
Wu Song Kills the Tiger 51
Fairytales from the Miao Tribe 52
Eight Immortals' Eight Treasures 54

Chapter 6   Children's World of Playing **55**
Children Setting Off Firecrackers 55
Girls Playing with Flute and Fan 57
Child Holding Lotus 58
May One Attain Boundless Happiness and Longevity — 59

Chapter 7   Continuous Well Wishing **60**
Continuous Auspicious Symbols 60
The Ba-Gua—The Eight Trigrams 62
Na-Ja 63
As You Wish—*Ru-yi* 65
The Revolving Pattern 66
Coins 67
The Longevity Lock 69

Lanterns 71
Human Figures 72
Auspicious Characters: Longevity, Health, Peace, and Fortune — 73
Abstract Motifs 75

Part II *Du Dou*– **The Undergarment**

Chapter 1   Stories from Chinese Opera **78**
Picking Up a Jade Bracelet and Kill the Dog to Warn the Wife — 78
Encounter with a Fairy 80
Rendezvous at Mulberry Garden 81
Oatmeal Canister 82

Chapter 2   Folktales and Fairytales **83**
Liu Hai Fishes for the Three-legged Toad 83
Tai-Chi 84
Ma Gu Presents Gift for Longevity 85

Chapter 3   Literary Symbolism **86**
Scholarly Pastimes 86
The Bamboo: A Scholar's Virtues 88

Chapter 4   The Joy of Love **89**
Mandarin Ducks Playing in the Water 89
The Phoenix and the Peony 90
Pomegranates: Many Children and grandchildren 91
The *Qi lin* 92
The Fairy Sends Baby 93
The Newlyweds' First Night 94

**Chapter 5   A Conglomeration of Splendid and
Beautiful Things** **95**
A Conglomeration of Splendid and Beautiful Things (1) — 95
A Conglomeration of Splendid and Beautiful Things (2) — 96

**Chapter 6   Auspicious Animals Sending Good
Tidings** **97**
The Green Lion 97
The Lion Playing with a Ball 99
The Crane: A Symbol for Longevity and the First Rank Civil Officer 100

**Chapter 7   To Hope One's Children Will Have a
Bright Future** **101**
Promotion Can Be Expected Very Soon 101

Chapter 8   Dispel Poison and Ward Off Evil **102**
The Five Poisons 102

Chapter 9   Undergarments (*Du Duo*) for Adults **104**
Undergarments for Adults 104

Spring 105
The Deer with White Spots: Longevity 106
The Lotus: Purity 107

Part III   Special Bibs

Chapter 1   To Contend in beauty and fascination ... **110**
Phoenix Brings Prosperity 110
Peach-shaped Bib 112
Butterfly-shaped Bib 113
Fruit-shaped Bib 114

Chapter 2   Bibs with Accessories **115**
Beautiful Tassels (1) 115
Beautiful Tassels (2) 117
Beautiful Tassels (3) 118
Luxurious Bibs (1) 119
Luxurious Bibs (2) 120
Luxurious Bibs (3) 121
Luxurious Bibs (4) 122

Chapter 3   Square Bibs **123**
Square Bibs (1) 123
Square Bibs (2) 124

Chapter 4   Bibs of Interest **125**
The Vest-style Bib (1) 125
The Vest-style Bib (2) 126
Special Bibs (1) 127
Special Bibs (2) 128
Special Bibs (3) 129

Part IV   Beautiful Exclamation – Capelets

Chapter 1   The Beauty of Design **132**
Elaborate Capelet 132
Butterfly Capelet 134
Peach Capelet 135
The Beauty of the Capelet (1) 136
The Beauty of the Capelet (2) 137
The Beauty of the Capelet (3) 138
Capelets for Adults (1) 139
Capelets for Adults (2) 140
Capelets for Adults (3) 141

Bibliography 142
About the Author and the Translators 143

目 次

はじめに **子供たちへ、よりすばらしい未来を** 35周年を迎え、「母の愛」という原点に立ち戻る —————————林泰生 **4**

まえがき **大きな愛情からなる小さな涎掛け** —————————————————————藍采如 **8**

第1部 幼児の第一枚目の衣装―涎掛け
第一章 山林に生息する動物 ————————— **16**
最も尊い地位の象徴――龍—————————————19
知恵の象徴――獅子紋————————————————22
威風堂々とした虎——————————————————26
世界平和を願う象の文様——————————————28
富の象徴―豚————————————————————29

第二章 水中に生息する動物 —————————— **30**
魚紋—————————————————————————31
赤ん坊―蛙————————————————————————32
試験合格―蟹————————————————————————33

第三章 舞い踊る蝶と蜂 ————————————— **34**
出世と富の象徴―鳥—————————————————35
夫婦円満の象徴―花と蝶——————————————38
動物の文様————————————————————————40

第四章 咲き誇る花 ——————————————— **41**
花の女王―牡丹——————————————————————41
厳寒に屈しない冬の梅——————————————————42
日々無事を祈る―四季平安————————————————43
咲き誇る花————————————————————————44
子孫繁栄を願う瓜の文様————————————————46
子沢山の瓢箪——————————————————————47
試験合格―連中三元————————————————————48

第五章 民間昔話と神話 ————————————— **49**
西遊記—————————————————————————49
虎と鷹に守られた龍の子の話————————————50
武松の虎退治——————————————————————51
苗族の神話————————————————————————53
仏教の宝物―八宝————————————————————54

第六章 遊びに興ずる子供たち ————————— **55**
嬰戯図その１―爆竹で遊ぶ子供たち—————————55
嬰戯図その2―笛や扇子で遊ぶ子供たち——————57
嬰戯図その3―蓮の花を持つ子供——————————58
嬰戯図その4―永遠の幸福と長寿——————————59

第七章 永遠の祝福 ——————————————— **60**
めでたい連続紋——————————————————————60
宇宙万物の変化を論ずる際の基本図形―八卦————62
哪吒—————————————————————————63
「如意雲」の文様———————————————————65
回字紋—————————————————————————66
銅銭紋—————————————————————————68
長生きを祈る錠——————————————————————70

灯篭紋—————————————————————————71
人間紋—————————————————————————72
めでたい四字熟語————————————————————74
抽象の図案————————————————————————75

第2部 恋物語にまつわる腹掛けの文様
第一章 恋物語 ————————————————— **78**
微笑ましい男女の出会い―拾玉鐲——————————79
中国版の竹取物語―天仙配——————————————80
２０年ぶりの夫婦再会―桑園会———————————81
村の女性に助けられた皇帝―麦仁缶—————————82

第二章 民間昔話と神話 ————————————— **83**
劉海仙人と蟾蜍の話———————————————————83
太極—————————————————————————84
西王母の誕生祝い―麻姑献寿————————————85

第三章 文人の嗜み ——————————————— **86**
文人の風雅な嗜み―琴、棋、書、畫—————————86
繁盛、節操、出世の象徴―竹————————————88

第四章 愛の喜び ——————————————— **89**
幸せそうに寄り添う鴛鴦―鴛鴦戯水—————————89
男女の愛情の象徴―鳳凰と牡丹———————————90
子沢山の石榴―子孫繁栄——————————————91
子供を運んでくれる麒麟―麒麟送子—————————92
子供を運んでくれる仙人―天仙送子—————————93
新婚初夜―洞房花燭夜———————————————————94

第五章 咲き誇る花 ——————————————— **95**
咲き誇る花その1—————————————————————95
咲き誇る花その2—————————————————————96

第六章 魔よけの青獅 ————————————— **97**
魔よけの青獅——————————————————————97
ボールで遊ぶ獅子―獅子戯球————————————99
長生きと出世の象徴―鶴————————————————100

第七章 光明吉祥の象徴―太陽 ———————— **101**
いつの日か必ず出世する―指日高昇—————————101

第八章 お守りとしての腹掛け ———————— **102**
魔よけのお札―五毒————————————————————102

第九章 大人の腹掛け ————————————— **104**
客家人の腹掛け——————————————————————104
春耕の場面―春耕図———————————————————105
長生きの象徴―梅花鹿——————————————————106
美しい蓮————————————————————————107

第3部 独特な形の涎掛け
第一章 奇をてらし、艶を競う ——————— **110**
鳳凰飛来―有鳳来儀———————————————————110
桃形の涎掛け——————————————————————112
蝶形の涎掛け——————————————————————113
果物の形の涎掛け————————————————————114

第二章 装飾的な涎掛け ———————————— **115**
美しい房飾りその1———————————————————115
美しい房飾りその2———————————————————117
美しい房飾りその3———————————————————118
華やかな涎掛けその1——————————————————119
華やかな涎掛けその2——————————————————120
華やかな涎掛けその3——————————————————121
華やかな涎掛けその4——————————————————122

第三章 四方形の涎掛け ———————————— **123**
方形の面白さその1———————————————————123
方形の面白さその2———————————————————124

第四章 面白い涎掛け ————————————— **125**
ベスト風の涎掛け————————————————————125
ベスト風の涎掛け―その2————————————————126
特殊な涎掛けその1———————————————————127
特殊な涎掛けその2———————————————————128
特殊な涎掛けその3———————————————————129

第4部 美しすぎるほどの肩掛け
第一章 造形の美 ——————————————— **132**
柳葉形の肩掛け——————————————————————132
蝶形の肩掛け——————————————————————134
桃形の肩掛け——————————————————————135
美しい肩掛けその1———————————————————136
美しい肩掛けその2———————————————————137
美しい肩掛けその3———————————————————138
大人の肩掛けその1———————————————————139
大人の肩掛けその2———————————————————140
大人の肩掛けその3———————————————————141

参考書目 —————————————————————————142
作者と訳者略歴 —————————————————————143

第 ① 部 幼兒的第一件衣裳—圍兜

Part I --- *Wei Zwei – The Bib*

最初章--- 幼児の第一枚目の衣装―涎掛け

第壹章

山林氤氳 Chapter 1 Powerful Animals
第一章 山林に生息する動物

① 非凡尊榮－**龍紋**

龍在古代傳說中由來已久，傳說中華民族的始祖伏羲和女媧的「蛇身」形象，是龍的原始形，夏禹的出世也與黃龍有關，因此在上古時代，龍已被當作祖神敬奉，中國人亦稱「龍的傳人」。

傳說中的龍，集中了許多動物的特點：鹿角、牛頭、蟒身、魚鱗、鷹爪，口角旁有鬚髯，頷下有珠，能巨能細，能幽能明，能喚雲作雨，降服妖魔，是英勇，權威與尊貴的象徵。歷代的皇帝，亦自稱為「真龍天子」，至今人們仍把龍看做是神聖吉祥的吉慶之物。

從古至今龍的造型經歷許多變化，在先秦之前：龍紋質樸粗獷，大多沒有肢爪，像爬蟲動物。＃1-1應該屬於較早期龍的形象，整隻龍成圓形環繞，稱為蟠龍，龍身綴有象徵吉祥如意的雲狀鎖片，猶如蟠龍在天，騰雲駕霧。此作品來自湖南苗漢不分的地區，長久以來一般多認為龍屬於漢族的圖騰，這件蟠龍圍兜，顯示在這苗漢不分的地區，苗族人長期受漢文化浸潤的影響。

龍的形象到了秦漢時期，多呈獸形，肢爪齊全，但無鱗甲，呈走龍狀。明代以後的龍：形象逐漸完善，至近代已豐富多彩了。總括來說，與龍有關的圖案，均有吉祥的涵意，常見的有「龍鳳呈祥」、「雙龍戲珠」等。

The Supreme Force—**The Dragon**

The dragon has always played a big role in ancient Chinese folklore. It is said that when the legendary Emperor Fu Xi and his successor sister Nü Wa took on appearances with human heads and snake-like tails, they were the origins of the dragon. Chinese people are often described to be "the descendents of the dragon."

The legendary dragon was made of cumulative qualities from various animals: the reins of a deer, the head of a bull, the scales of a fish, and the claws of an eagle. The dragon was the spirit of change—it could make itself visible or invisible, it could summon the clouds and the rain, and its power was so awesome that all other creatures yielded in its presence. Emperors used to call themselves "the true prince of the dragon," therefore, the dragon has always been considered to be the most fortunate and powerful of symbols.

From the past until the present, the shape and appearance of the dragon have experienced many changes. Prior to the Qin Dynasty(221-206 B.C.), the dragon had a rough exterior and didn't really have limbs, so it crawled on the ground like an insect. Figure 1-1 depicts a dragon from this period. The whole dragon forms a circle and is called the *Pan* dragon, or the curled-up dragon. On its body are cloud-like scales that symbolize good fortune, as if the dragon were riding the clouds up in the heaven. This bib is from Hunan Province, in an area where there is little distinction between the Han and Miao minority group. Because the dragon has long been considered to be a distinctly Han symbol, this bib shows that the Miaos have been deeply influenced by the Hans.

Fig . #1-1

＃1-2是以貼布繡來表現的「雙龍戲珠」，龍身鱗片以多種弧形色塊拼貼出層次感，讓整個圍兜顯得色彩斑斕，童趣十足。值得欣賞的是＃1-2龍的雙眼繡工精細，以貼布創造出一圈一圈的立體效果，靈活俏皮的眼神，果然應了俗諺所說：「畫龍點睛」，為這幅雙龍戲珠的圍兜增添不少可看性。

＃1-3中左手邊的龍屬於回首龍，以黑色絨布為襯底，益發襯托出龍的華麗與貴氣，龍的上方還繡有做工精細的蝴蝶與蜘蛛，呈現出苗族人家想像中的大自然景象。

＃1-4做工細緻華麗，判斷極可能是皇室中皇子的用品。這件作品完全依循皇室的規格，圍兜的面上和皇帝的龍袍一樣，繡上了代表天子尊榮的龍形圖騰，（包括左右及中央各一條龍），以及山形、水紋及雲飾，極為尊貴，而全部圖飾均以金線繡成，與金黃色的底相輝映，更凸顯了華麗感，也彰顯了皇室獨一無二的地位。

In Figure 1-2, using the appliqué technique, is a depiction of the Chinese saying, "two dragons playing with a pearl," which represents a sense of power. The dragon's scales are made of different colored appliqués that are attached in an overlapping fashion, which gives the dragon a 3-D effect. It is worthy of noting that the dragon's eyes in Figure 1-2 are made of tiny adjacent embroidered circles that make the eyes of the dragon pop with liveliness. There is a Chinese saying that when dragons are painted, they are never finished until the eyes are drawn. In that last stroke when the dragon's eyes are drawn, the dragon would vividly come alive—this is never truer than in this bib.

In Figure 1-3, the dragon on the left turns its head backward to look at the dragon next to it. The black background gives the whole image a regal beauty. Above the dragons are butterflies and spiders.

The handiwork in Figure 1-4 is especially intricate, and judging by its design, it probably came from the palace. The dragons on this bib are stitched in the same way dragons on the emperor's robe would have been stitched. In addition, the mountain formations, the water ripples, and the clouds all mimic designs from an emperor's robe (water, mountain, and cloud patterns symbolize the power to rule and bring great order to a country). The gold threads and the deep yellow background also denote a sense of majesty and nobility.

Fig . #1-2

Fig・#1-3

最も尊い地位の象徴―龍

龍に関する話は古代から伝えられ、漢民族の祖先「伏羲」と「女媧」は、蛇の形をしており、それが即ち龍の原型と考えられています。中国最初の帝王「夏」と「禹」の生まれも、黄龍と関連があると言われ、そのため、龍は祖先神として崇められ、中国人は『龍の子孫』とも呼ばれるようになったのです。

伝説の中の龍は、様々な動物の特徴を合わせ持っています。例えば龍には、鹿の角、牛の頭、蛇の体、魚の鱗、鷹の爪が

有り、口元に髭、顎の下に玉を持ち、体は大きくもなれば、小さくもなり、また姿を変幻自在に変えることができ、雲を呼んだり、雨を降らせたりもします。そして妖怪魔物を降伏させる強い力を持っているため、勇敢、権威、高貴の象徴となりました。歴代の皇帝は、自らを龍から生まれ変わった統治者と称し、また人々は龍を神聖で吉祥の象徴としてきました。

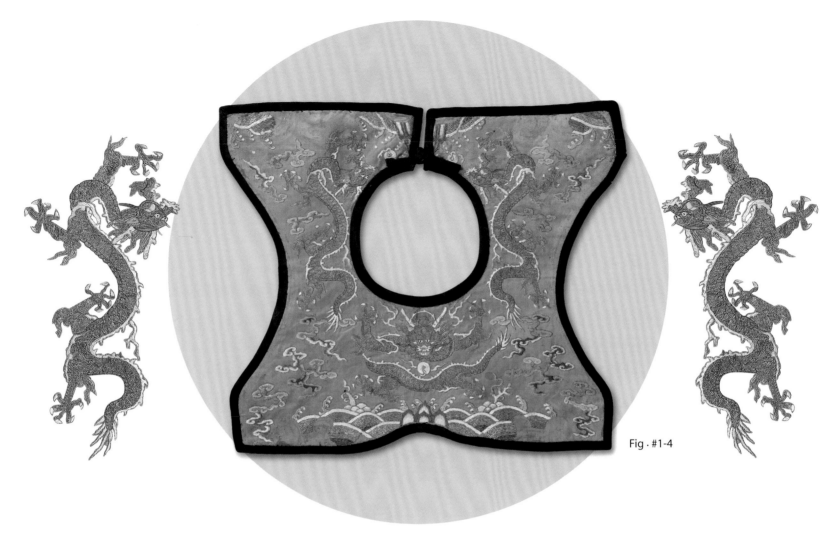

Fig · #1-4

昔から龍は、前に述べた特徴を持っていながら、形状的に多くの変化を遂げてきました。2、3千年ほど前の殷、周などの時代には、龍は素朴で豪放な形をしていました、まるで蛇のようで、足も爪もありませんでした。#1-1は比較的に初期の龍の形をしています。体全体でとぐろを巻いており、「蟠龍」と呼ばれます。全身にめでたい意味を持つ雲状の鱗を付けており、雲の間を縫いながら空を飛んでいます。この作品は、湖南の苗族と漢民族が入り混じった土地から来たものです。昔から一般の人は、龍は漢民族を代表する文様と考えていたため、この「蟠龍」文様の涎掛けは、漢苗雑居の地域において、苗族が長期的に漢民族の影響を受けていることが見受けられます。

#1-2はアップリケの刺繍で、二匹の龍が一つの玉で戯れ、遊んでいる様子を表しています。体の鱗は布切れでアップリケ風に縫い付けて、色の濃淡を出しており、色鮮やかで可愛らしく。二つの目はアップリケによって立体的な効果が出ており、生き生きとしています。#1-3は、左側の龍は後ろを振り返る姿から「回首龍」と呼ばれます。黒のビロード地で華やかな感じを出しています。なお、龍の上の方には蝶と蜘蛛の刺繍があり、苗族の人々が見た昆虫の世界を表しています。

#1-4は大変精緻で華麗な作りになっており、皇太子が使った物ではないかと思われます。涎掛けの表面には、天子の崇高な地位を代表する龍や山、波、雲の文様が施され、皇帝が着る「龍袍」という服との文様と変わりません。これら全ての文様は金の糸で刺繍され、黄色い生地と共に輝き、皇室ならではの豪華さを表しています。

② 智慧的象徵 – 獅紋

獅子其實並非源自中國，但是獅子在民間文化中卻到處可見。最明顯的例子就是過年時的舞獅，為吉祥的象徵，也因獅子凶猛威風，因此人們以它驅邪避祟。還有常見的大獅小獅，即是「太師少保」的意思，與「朝中當官」或「官運亨通」有相同的寓意。另外，獅子在佛教中也有特殊的寓意，代表「智慧」的文殊菩薩騎著獅子，即象徵「神聖」與「吉祥」。

在圍兜作品中，虎紋是最常見的紋飾，反倒是獅紋相當少見。# 2-1為相當罕見的雙獅圖騰圍兜，上頭的獅子造型特殊而繁複，首先是布折疊出的眼睛和牙齒，十分立體活潑，額上有瑞雲形象的如意雲紋，象徵吉祥如意；此外，獅子的眼、腳、尾還以抽紗手法製造出鬚鬚的特殊效果，尾巴也不是寫實的模樣，而是像傘狀般散開，恰似一片樹葉，做工十分精細。

Symbol of Intelligence – **The Lion**

Though the lion does not originate from China, its image is often seen throughout Chinese culture. The most familiar example is the dancing lion that comes out during the Lunar New Year celebrations. Lions symbolize good luck, and, because they are strong and menacing in nature, they also symbolize the power to repel evil. The lion is often found at the entrance of Buddhist temples because it represents wisdom, and Buddhist deities that are depicted mounted on the lion represent saintliness and valor.

On bibs, it is much more common to see tigers depicted, whereas the lion is depicted less frequently. Therefore, the design in Figure 2-1 is a rare example of twin lions sewn onto a bib. The lions here are made using very complicated techniques. The eyes and the teeth are both sewn on with folded pieces of fabric, giving those features a three-dimensional effect. On the forehead of the lions are cloud motifs, which are symbols of luck. The "fur" on the lion is lifelike, composed of brushed-out threads, but the tail is more abstract in its design with the leaf-like veins along the inside.

Though this is not a contemporary piece of work, the use of contrasting colors—red and green—is very audacious and modern. You can imagine that the mother sewing this bib was perhaps hoping for a rambunctious and energetic child.

Figure 2-2 shows an exquisite bib that, each time you look at it, becomes all the more alluring. The black edge coupled with the golden threading immediately catches the eye. And all the beasts that are embroidered using the knot stitch, such as the lion and the tiger, seem to come alive with animal spirit.

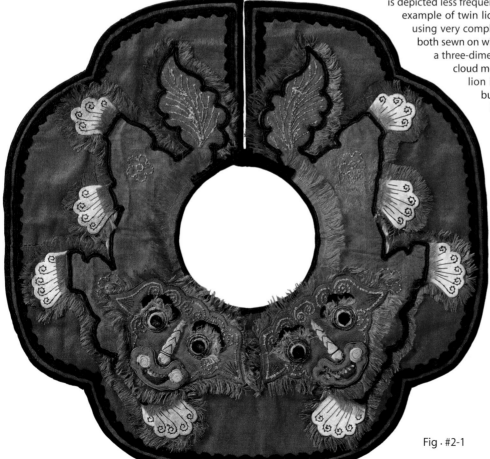

Fig . #2-1

＃2-2的圍兜，繡工與布料均極為細緻講究，是集華麗與工藝之美於一身的顛峰作品，值得細細品味與欣賞。這只圍兜，利用黑邊與金色的繡線交織，第一眼就緊緊捉住人的目光；細部欣賞，面上利用打籽繡技法鏽出的多隻吉獸，包括獅、麒麟、老虎與鹿，無不細膩華麗，靈活靈現，充分展露了中國刺繡的工藝顛峰。

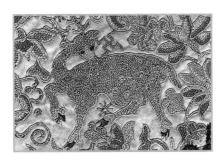

Fig．#2-2

知恵の象徴—獅子紋

中国に獅子がいるわけではありませんが、民俗文化の中では随所に見られます。例えば獅子舞は縁起物ばかりでなく、その威風堂々とした姿が邪悪を追い払うことができると、民間では信じてきました。またよく見かける大、小の獅子の組み合わせの飾りは、出世を願う意味を持っています。さらに仏教では獅子は特別な意味を持っており、例えば知恵の代表である文殊菩薩は、獅子に乗っていて、神聖と吉祥の意味を持っています。

涎掛けの作品の中で、虎の文様は大変よく見かけますが、獅子はそうでもありません。#2-1は、二頭の獅子の文様で飾った涎掛けで、大変珍しいものです。獅子の造形は複雑で難しく、まず目と牙を布で折って作り、立体的で生き生きとした姿を現し、額には雲の形をした文様で「吉祥如意」の祝福が込められています。その他、獅子の目、足、尻尾は、ドローン．ワーク(Drawn work)という技法で毛のふわふわした感じを上手く表しています。また尻尾は開いた傘のように一枚の木の葉の形をしており、細かい工夫が施されています。

この作品は年代が古いのにもかかわらず、赤と緑の色の使い方は相当大胆で、若い母親のはつらつとした豊富な美意識を伝えています。

#2-2の涎掛けは、刺繍も生地も大変上等なもので、見る人の目を十分に楽しませてくれます。刺繍の細かいところをよく見ると、ノット．ステッチ(Knot stitch)という技法が採られていることが判ります。文様として、縁起の良い動物、例えば獅子、キリン、虎、鹿などの姿が、どれも細緻にして華麗で生き生きとしています。中国刺繍工芸の頂点を見せられた思いです。

③

虎虎生風－**虎紋**

虎是百獸之王，因其威武勇猛，而且中國古代敬虎為神，被列為四方神之一。虎神能驅妖鎮宅，祛邪避災，在許多地方特別是黃河流域一帶，人們喜歡讓小孩穿戴虎頭鞋、虎頭帽、虎頭圍嘴等，希望老虎能保護小孩順利長大。虎紋的衣飾以虎鞋最多，而又因老虎威風凜凜，多數在男孩兒的衣帽上見此美麗的虎紋。

＃3-1是一件繡工細緻的四片虎圍兜，自山西收集而來，四個布片，出自母親特出的設計美感，加上細緻的繡工，尤其別緻。四隻橘黃夾雜的小虎，用色鮮豔活潑，使得四隻小虎少了張牙舞爪的凶猛，反倒較像家中溫馴可愛的小貓咪。作品運用了挖雲、貼布與立體高繡等多種技巧，做工相當繁複，小老虎的眼珠並以穿孔小琉璃點綴而成，在夜裡小眼珠閃啊閃的，真的很可愛。

＃3-2的用色相當漂亮，深藍色的底將豔紅色的虎襯的更加華麗。雙虎的虎頭是這只圍兜的視覺重點，用心縫製的母親用了相當細膩的技巧，包括高繡和貼布來呈現虎頭的立體感，值得細細品味。另外，虎牙的作法也值得欣賞，需先把布條折疊、堆高、打硬，再縫起來，母親的細心巧手處處流露對孩兒的無限疼愛。

老虎護衛人們，中國人也特別喜愛在節慶時以虎紋來做裝飾。早期端午節時，人們用艾草編虎，或用彩紙剪虎，掛貼於門上，叫做「艾虎」，藉以逐疫除災；春節時，也在門上畫虎，或在廳堂掛上「鎮宅神虎」圖，希望老虎鎮守家宅財富，使妖魔鬼魅不敢來侵擾，保佑家人平安健康。

在＃3-3中，可以看到老虎的口中啣著艾草，就是所謂的「艾虎」，也稱為「虎口生花」。而這件作品的立體造型和葉狀虎尾，也是欣賞的重點。＃3-4的虎身同樣也綴以艾草，金線壓邊和挖雲、貼布的設計，顯得相當多彩可愛。

Fig . #3-1

23

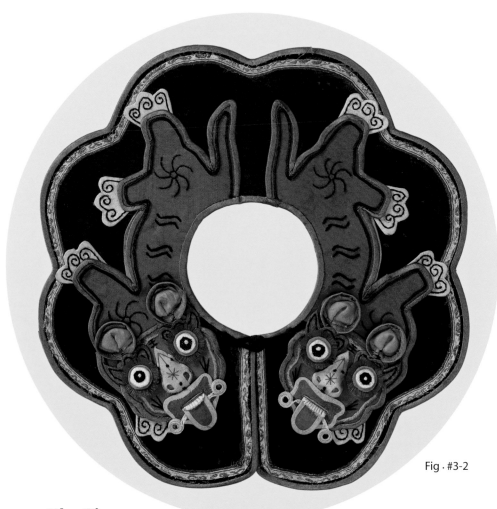

Fig · #3-2

Lively and Vigorous—**The Tiger**

The tiger is considered the Chinese king of the wild beasts. It is one of the four animals symbolizing power and energy (the other three being the elephant, the leopard, and the lion). It is readily accepted as the model for courage and is an emblem of terror and danger. Adults like to dress their children in clothing with images of tigers on them in hopes that the tiger will protect them all throughout childhood. It is perhaps more common to see tigers on little boys' clothes than on girls'.

Figure 3-1 shows a bib with quadruplet tigers; it is from the Shanxi area. The four orange tigers lack the teeth of more menacing tigers, so they look instead like gentle kittens. Although the tigers are cute and have a simple look, the bib actually uses many different techniques, such as open-work and raised embroidery, which are both very complicated. The eyes of the little tigers are actually made of ancient glass and, in the dark, they even sparkle.

The use of color in Figure 3-2 is especially beautiful—the navy background really makes the red in the foreground pop. The heads of these twin tigers are the main focus of this bib. The mother used

very advanced techniques, such as raised embroidery and appliqué, to give the heads a three-dimensional look. Also, the method of making the teeth is worthy of noting: she had to first fold strips of cloth, repeatedly applying glue to the strips to harden the cloth, and then sew each tooth onto the bib.

Chinese people like to use tiger motifs on clothing for special occasions. During Dragon Boat Festivals in the early days, people used *moxa* grass and made it into tiger shapes. They also made paper cut-outs of tigers and pasted them onto doors as a means of protection. During the Chinese Lunar New Year, they would make drawings of tigers on the doors, hoping that the tigers would ward off evil and bring the family good health and keep them safe.

In Figure 3-3, you can see that this tiger has some *moxa* grass in his mouth. This is known as the "*moxa* grass tiger." The leaf-like tail of this tiger is of particular interest in this piece. The body of the tiger in Figure 3-4 also resembles the shape of a leaf. The gold outline and open work design make this an especially adorable tiger.

Fig . #3-3

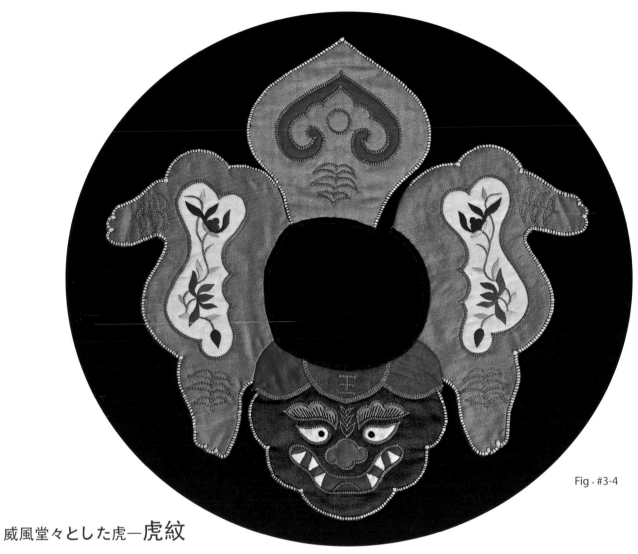

Fig . #3-4

威風堂々とした虎—**虎紋**

虎は百獣の王で、その威風により、中国古代から神として敬われ、「四方の神」の一つとされました。虎の神は妖怪を制し、災難を追い払ってくれると人々は信じていました。特に黄河流域一帯の人々は、子供に虎の文様を刺繍した靴、帽子、涎掛けを着用させ、子供の無事成長を願いました。虎の飾りは靴に一番よく見られますが、あの威風堂々とした姿は特に男児に人気が有り、男の子の衣服、帽子にその美しい刺繍の文様を見ることができます。

#3-1は4枚の刺繍のある涎掛けで、山西から収集したものです。4枚の布は母親がデザインして細かく刺繍した大変特別な作品です。4匹の橙色の子虎は、鮮やかな彩りのせいか、家の中で飼われているおとなしく可愛い子猫のように見えます。オープン.ワーク.エンブロイダリー(Open work embroidery)、アップリケや立体刺繍などの様々な特殊で手の込んだ技法によって作られ、目玉にはガラス玉が嵌められ、夜になると輝きがよりいっそう可愛らしく見えます。

#3-2の色使いは大変上手で、深い藍の生地の上に濃い赤の虎の体がとても映えています。虎の頭がポイントで、母親は立体感を出すことに苦心したと見受けられます。その他、虎の牙の縫い方も面白く、注目すべきところです。虎は人間を守ってくれると信じられており、中国人は祭日や節句などに、虎の文様を飾る慣わしがあります。

また昔の人々は、端午の節句に蓬(よもぎ)で虎を編んだり、色紙で虎の切り絵を作って玄関の門に飾り、厄払いをしていました。またお正月には、虎の絵を描いて客間の壁に貼り付け、悪魔を追い払い、家財や家族の健康を守ってもらおうとしました。

#3-3は、口に蓬(よもぎ)を銜えた虎で、その立体的な造形や、葉の形をした尻尾が珍しいです。

#3-4も同様、全身に艾草(もぐさ)を縫い付け、金の糸で縁を作ったアップリケのデザインが多彩で可愛らしいです。

太瓶有象－象、鹿、牛紋

「太瓶有象」這句話是從「太平無象」一詞而來，在古書《資治通鑑》中曾提到「太平無象」以諷刺統治者粉飾太平，並表示太平盛世並無一定標誌，因此，後來以花瓶與象的結合，寓意世界美好。在台北故宮博物院就有以琺瑯製作非常精美的「太瓶有象」作品，即一隻象背上馱著一只花瓶。

此外，象體大力壯，性情卻溫馴，傳說中，它能預兆靈瑞，也只有在有賢君時，靈象才會出現，因此象是吉祥的象徵。

鹿在傳說中常為仙人所騎，也說鹿、鶴同時衛護靈芝仙草，所以，鹿是象徵長壽的仙獸。此外，「鹿」與「祿」音同，表示福氣、俸祿之意，在吉祥語中，一百頭鹿稱「百祿」，當蝙蝠與鹿同時出現時稱「福祿雙全」，常見鹿口中啣著一隻靈芝草，也因鹿的全身皆可入藥，中國人相信鹿茸為滋補珍品，因此中國人常說「鹿壽千歲」，相信鹿可為人類增長壽命。

牛是十二生肖之一，神話中，道家的老子就是騎著青牛要經過涵谷關時，守關的小吏看到有紫氣東來，因此知道老子是仙人便攔住他。老子知道這名小吏已經看出他的真面目，便把《道德經》傳授給他。此外，在農耕社會，牛象徵「春天」，並為農人所崇拜尊敬，春節時常常見到「春牛圖」，並傳說牛與水旱有關，有些地方，將石頭或青銅做的牛塑像投入水中，傳說有防止水患的功能。

＃4-1的圍兜，上頭以貼布繡的手法繡以牛、象、虎等象徵吉祥的動物，是來自湖南的民間作品。

＃4-2同樣綴有象、鹿、麒麟等動物，取「太瓶有象」、「福祿雙全」之意，紅色襯底的絨布，襯托得作品洋溢著喜氣洋洋的過節氣氛。

Signs of Peace —**The Elephant, the Deer, and the Ox**

The elephant, along with the tiger, leopard, and lion, is one of the four animals that represent strength and power. But the elephant is also known to be gentle and intuitive, so it has the connotation of good luck and peace.

The deer is said to be ridden by immortals and, because deer are thought to have a very long life, they are also the symbol of longevity. The pronunciation of deer in Chinese is the same for the word, *lu*, which means having the luck to serve in the high court; so the deer also has the connotation of good fortune. When the deer appears together with the bat (*fu*, in Chinese also denoting luck), it is doubly lucky.

The ox is one of the twelve zodiac signs. In agricultural circles, the ox symbolizes spring. The ox is often used in ceremonial plowing and is an indication of the coming of spring.

The bib in Figure 4-1 bears appliqués of all auspicious animals—the elephant, the ox, and the tiger. It is from Hunan Province.

Figure 4-2 is similar in its depiction of auspicious animals—the elephant, the deer, and the *qi lin*, which is a mythical, deer-like animal. The *qi lin*, along with elephants, are said to appear only in time of peace and prosperity.

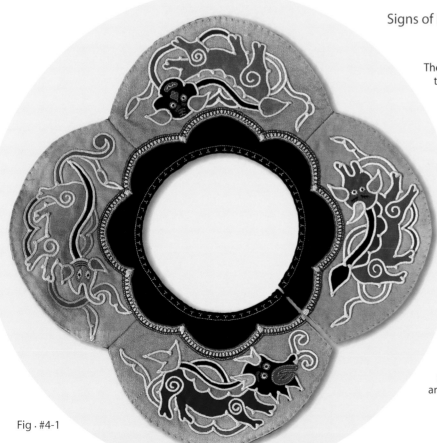

Fig . #4-1

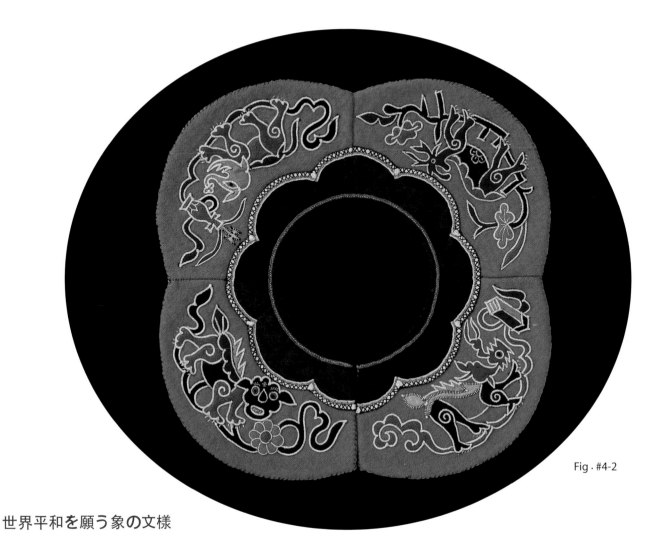

Fig . #4-2

世界平和を願う象の文様

「太平」の「平」と花瓶の「瓶」の中国語の発音は同じですので、「平」は花瓶として、また「有象」は象として、この二つを組み合わせて「世界平和」の意味を表しています。台北の故宮博物院には、七宝焼きの非常に精緻な「太平有象」の作品を所蔵しており、その象の背中には花瓶が乗っています。

この他、象は体が大きく力もあるが、性格は温厚なので、言い伝えの中では瑞祥とされてきました。優れた帝王が世に現れる時にだけ、「霊象」は姿を見せると信じられ、吉祥の象徴とされました。

鹿は言い伝えの中で仙人が乗る動物であるとされ、口に一葉の霊芝仙草を銜えているのがよく見かけられるのは鶴と共に、不老長寿の薬「霊芝仙草」を守るとされているからです。そのため、鹿は長生きの象徴でもありました。鹿はまた「禄」という、出世を意味する言葉と同音なので、百匹の鹿は人に大出世を祝福するめでたい贈り物として使われてきました。蝙蝠は幸せの「福」と同音なので、蝙蝠(コウモリ)と鹿が対の文様は「福禄双全」として、出世すると共に幸せでありますように、とい

う意味が込められています。鹿は体全体が漢方薬になり、特に中国人は鹿の角を体力作りに最もよい栄養剤と信じています。

牛は十二支の一つで、昔道教の創始者老子という人が乗っていたと言われています。農耕社会で牛は春を象徴し、農民に愛されてきました。お正月になると、至るところで、牛の絵が一年分の暦と共に印刷され、家々の壁に飾っていました。またある地方では、石か青銅で作られた牛の像を水中に投げ入れると、水害を免れるという言い伝えも残っています。

#4-1の涎掛けは、湖南から収集した民間の作品で、上の方はアップリケで牛、象、虎などの動物を刺繍したもので、首に掛ける部分は、花びらの造形をしており中々優雅なものです。

#4-2も同様、象、鹿、キリンなどの動物で「太平有象」「福禄双全」のめでたい意味を出しています。首に掛ける部分は花びら型で美しく、生地は赤のビロードで喜ばしい雰囲気を醸し出しています。

⑤

知足常樂－**豬形圍兜**

豬是大家非常熟悉的動物，在尋常百姓生活中扮演了相當重要的角色，或許它並不尊榮，卻是最溫馴和親切的動物，正代表了平民百姓衣食無缺的歡樂生活，和知足常樂的人生態度。

＃5的圍兜就做成一隻小豬的模樣，看起來既可愛又討人喜歡。縫製這只豬形圍兜的年輕母親發揮了豐富的想像力，創造出卡通化的小豬造型，瞧，圓圓的大眼睛，紅色的豬鼻子，葉片狀白色勾邊的耳朵，再加上尾端長了鬃的豬尾巴，真的是很可愛。這位母親還運用了白色細線，在黑底的小豬身上繡出一根根的白色細毛，讓這只豬形圍兜顯得更加活潑與生動。

Contentment Brings Happiness—**The Pig**

The pig is a familiar animal for all; and in the lives of everyday people, it plays a similar role: it is a simple, unadorned animal that is gentle in nature and represents the complacency and happiness of everyday life.

The pig in Figure 5 looks almost like a cartoon with its big round eyes, red nose, leaf-shaped ears, and whisker-like tail. Here, the mother used a black background to show off the tiny little white hairs that she carefully stitched.

富の象徴—**豚**

豚は誰もが知っている動物で、庶民の生活の中では重要な役割をしています。派手なイメージこそありませんが、そのふくよかな外見とおっとりした性格から、満ち足りた楽しい生活の象徴になりました。

#5の涎掛けは可愛い子豚の形をしており、若い母親がその豊富な想像力を働かせ、作り出した漫画のような子豚です。真ん丸い目、赤い鼻、葉の形をした耳、毛を生やした尻尾の可愛いこと。この母親はまた白い細かい糸で、黒地の体に一本ずつ細い毛を刺繍したので、子豚を一層生き生きと可愛く見せています。

Fig . #5

水波蕩漾 Chapter 2 Auspicious Aquatic Animals
第二章 水中に生息する動物

第壹部 幼兒的第一件衣裳—圍兜

⑥

年年有餘 – 魚紋

「魚」與「餘」同音，所以「魚」象徵富足有餘。在吉祥的圖案中，魚和蓮花出現時，就是「年年有餘」（蓮蓮有魚）的寓意，而「鮎」的諧音也是「年」，所以如果有兩條鮎魚，再加上金黃色的橘子，就是「年年大吉」。在黃河流域（特別是陝北、陝西一帶），民間流傳「魚戲蓮」的圖案，則暗藏著生殖與求偶的隱喻意義。

#6-1是採集自安徽的作品，這件幼兒圍兜上繡有龍頭形象的魚。一般若出現龍頭形象的魚，有蘊含「魚龍變化」的意義，這句流傳民間的吉祥話語，表示人不發跡只因時運未濟，有待來日必定能一躍龍門而飛騰成龍。它也是對有志者的吉祥祝福。若出現鯉魚躍龍門，則是隱喻科舉高中之意。

這件圍兜在靠近頸項處以圈金的方式勾出輪廓，加上魚龍變化的吉祥語，襯上亮麗的紅底，充滿富貴吉慶之氣。尤其是部分刺繡以破絲繡來表現，使整件圍兜呈現出柔潤的光澤，就像溫柔的慈暉。可以想見，當寶寶穿戴起來，透過皮膚非常柔細的觸感，更能處處感受到母愛的溫柔光輝。

#6-2是繡著長長鬍鬚的美麗鮎魚，以緊密的鎖繡呈現做工的精細，並綴有娃娃魚，模樣非常可愛。

#6-3中的雙魚，以貼布繡和特殊的抽紗繡技法來表現，在魚翅和魚尾部分呈現輕盈朦朧的美感，色彩的配置也很繽紛亮麗，並綴以長長的鬍鬚，有「金玉滿堂」（金魚滿塘）的吉祥意味。

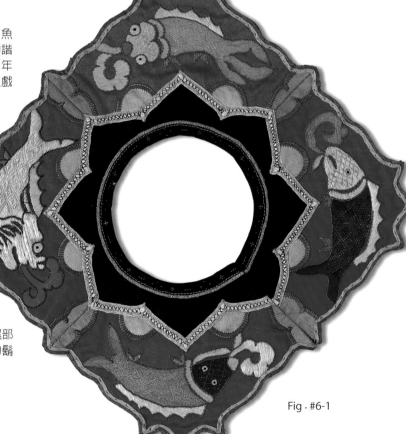

Fig · #6-1

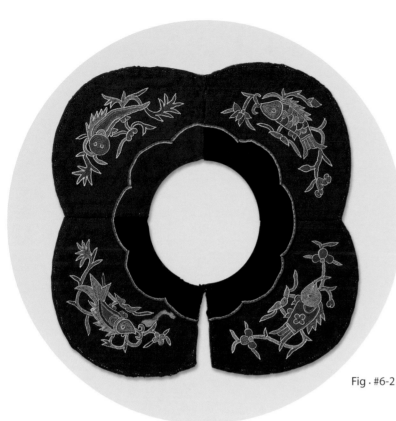

Fig・#6-2

Fig・#6-3

Surplus and Abundance Every Year—**The Fish**

Because the pronunciation of "fish" (*yu*) and "excess" (*yu*) are the same in Chinese, fish has always been the symbol of wealth and abundance.

The bib in Figure 6-1 comes from Anhui. Of interest here is the fish with the dragon's head. It is a depiction of a Chinese saying that if a carp can swim against the current of the river and jump over the Dragon Gate of Yellow River, then the carp will turn into a dragon. This saying is used to describe a scholar who has passed the examination of the civil service.

The fish in Figure 6-2 are called *nian*, which is also the way "year" is pronounced in Chinese. And because the pronunciation of "fish" is the same as "excess" or "abundance," this particular fish is a hope that every year, one will enjoy abundance and wealth.

The double fish in Figure 6-3 are whiskered goldfish that are an especially auspicious type of fish in Chinese culture. The stitching techniques used here give the fish a feeling of movement that is quite remarkable.

年々有り余る程の富—魚

中国では、「魚」と「余」とは同音なので、魚で「富が有り余る」ことを象徴しています。#6-1の涎掛けの首周りは、ゴールド．エンブロイダリー(Gold embroidery)という技法で輪郭を出し、その上に鯉の登竜門にまつわるめでたい文様を加え、赤の生地で品良く慶びの雰囲気を漂わせています。また一部にスプリット．シルク．ステッチ(Split silk stitch)を施し、この涎掛けに優しく柔らかい感触を与えています

#6-2はチェーン．ステッチ．エンブロイダリー(Chain stitch embroidery)という大変緻密な技法で、とても長いひげをした美しい鮎の刺繍文様が施された涎掛けで、可愛い山椒魚が一匹混じっています。

#6-3の二匹の魚はアップリケなどの技法で表現されています。色鮮やかな尾ひれは、今にも軽やかに動き出しそうな感じがします。色の工夫も印象に残る作品です。

⑦

蟾蜍坐蓮—**蛙紋**

中國北方人民喜歡蛙，因與「娃」同音，有時將青蛙繡在娃娃的圍兜和肚兜上，或把娃娃的枕頭做成蛙形，讓可愛又吉祥的青蛙陪著娃娃甜蜜入眠。#7是收集自浙江的作品，裡頭繡有兩蛙三蟹，充分表現母親對孩兒未來的殷殷期待，繡工也相當細緻。這只圍兜不僅圖案可愛，桃紅、湛藍、鮮橘與黃色混搭的效果也很鮮豔明亮。

Wa Wa—**The Frog**

Northerners are particularly fond of frogs because the pronunciation of "frog"(*wa*) is the same as that for "baby" (*wa wa*). For that reason, it is common to see images of frogs embroidered onto babies' bibs and shirts. The bib in Figure 7 is from Zhejiang —there are two frogs and three crabs on it. The needlework here is very delicate and the colors are bright and innocent.

赤ん坊—**蛙**

中国の北の方では、「蛙」は赤ん坊を意味する「娃」と同音なので、蛙も好んで、よく涎掛けや金太郎掛けなどの刺繍飾りにされます。また蛙の形をした枕も作られました。#7は浙江からのもので、蛙2匹とカニ3匹の文様が施されています。この作品は、文様が可愛いばかりでなく、鮮やかな桃色、青が用いられ、黄色との対比による効果も印象的です。

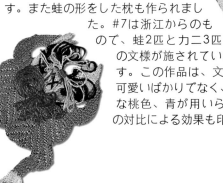

Fig．#7

科舉高中－**蟹紋**

蟹為有甲的動物，「甲」是古時科舉的名稱，科舉制度分為鄉試、會試、殿試，而殿試又有三甲之分，取一甲前三名（狀元、榜眼、探花）之後，再取兩甲，寓意科舉高中。#8為收集自陝北地方的圍兜，面上繡有五隻靈活生動的螃蟹，即為典型的蟹紋，母親希望藉由吉祥的蟹紋，為尚未長大的孩童無限祝福，盼來日科舉高中，仕途光明。

Crab

Crabs have shells, and crab shells are pronounced *jia*, which is synonymous with a successful candidate in the imperial examination under the former civil service system. The bib in Figure 8, from northern Shanxi, has five lively crabs embroidered on it. The mother here is hoping that her child will grow up to enjoy endless fortune and have a bright educational and professional future.

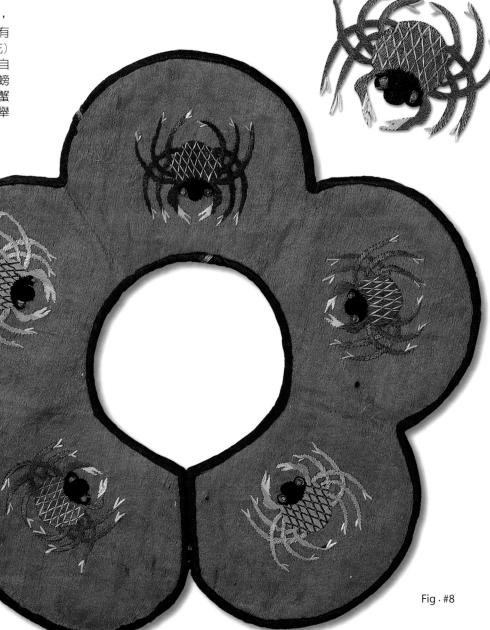

Fig.#8

試験合格－蟹

昔中国では「科挙」という人材登用のための試験がありました。「甲」は科挙関連用語の一つであります。甲羅がある蟹を文様にした贈り物は、「試験合格」という願いが込められています。#8は陝北地方から収集したもので、5匹の蟹が刺繍してあり、将来出世するようにというわが子への祝福が伺えます

第 參 章

蝶亂蜂喧 Chapter 3 Busybees—Birds and InsectsAnimals
第三章 舞い踊る蝶と蜂

⑨
功名富貴 – 鳥紋

鳥，常見在吉祥語之中。古時，公雞鳴啼報曉，天際將亮，寓意前途光明，而「公」雞「鳴」啼，即是「功名」，而公雞旁邊又添加牡丹，牡丹為富貴花，所以有祝頌人學業、事業成功，仕途康莊，名利雙收之意。

此外，傳說喜鵲具有預兆的神異本領，而且民間傳說中有牛郎織女藉由喜鵲搭橋進行鵲橋會的動人故事，因此，喜鵲在民間是吉祥報喜的鳥兒，多與梅花搭配成為「喜鵲登梅」，也有「喜上眉（梅）梢」之意，而梅花又稱報春花，也稍來春意浪漫的喜訊。若以白鷺鷥搭配蓮花為主題，即「一鷺蓮（連）科」，古時考試若連續考中謂之「連科」，「一路連科」即指仕途順遂，考試連捷。

＃9-1收集自陝西一帶，上頭精心繡製的各種鳥類圖案，即為典型的「功名富貴」、「喜鵲登梅」、「一路連科」，活靈活現的鳥兒與美麗的花朵，處處流露母親對孩兒滿滿的祝福。這件圍兜以正紅的底色，在鳥身上襯上做工繁複的破絲繡，呈現極為圓潤的光澤，其他部分則為繁瑣的鎖繡，細膩的繡工尤其值得欣賞。

＃9-2以貼布繡來表現鳳凰的吉慶之氣。在古代神話中，雄稱「鳳」，雌為「凰」，傳說此鳥可帶來和平，是幸福吉祥的瑞鳥，在歷代的王朝中，以帝為龍，后為鳳，為鳥中之王，其美麗的形象廣為民間所喜愛，有鳳求凰的故事流傳和「鳳凰于飛」的吉祥話，也稱之為「仁鳥」。這件圍兜的色彩極為豐富，令人賞心悅目。

＃9-3為河南漢族的作品，繡的是另一種瑞鳥––綬帶鳥。以「壽」站立在山茶花（春天開的報春花）之上，用來寓意「春光長壽」。

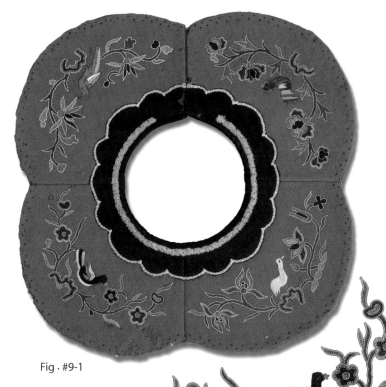

Fig . #9-1

第壹部 幼兒的第一件衣裳─圍兜

Laurel Achievement and Rich Life—**The Bird**

All kinds of birds are auspicious in Chinese culture. Because the rooster makes the morning call, it has the connotation of bringing on a bright future. Especially when coupled with the peony, which is a flower of elegance and class, the rooster bestows upon its wearer a good future in education and business.

The magpie is also considered a lucky bird. In Chinese, it is literally the "bird of joy." Chinese people love the sounds the magpie makes, and it is good fortune when magpies nest near a person's home. When an image of the magpie is paired with an image of the plum blossom (which symbolizes the coming of spring), it symbolizes happiness and romance. If the image is of an egret and the lotus flower, then there is the wish for success in schooling.

The bib in Figure 9-1 is from the Shanxi region and is filled with the mother's hopes and dreams for her baby's success in the future. There is a blue magpie on the bottom left of the collar and an egret on the bottom right of the collar. Against the deep red backdrop, the refined chain stitching on the little birds' bodies gives them an iridescent sheen.

In Figure 9-2, we see the phoenix, which is the most highly regarded bird of all because, next to the dragon, the phoenix is the queen. It is also the bird of peace.

In Figure 9-3, there is another kind of auspicious long-tailed bird. The long tail represents longevity.

Fig . #9-2

出世と富の象徴—鳥

鳥はめでたい言葉の中に度々入っています。夜明けに雄「鶏」が「鳴」いて日の出を告げることから、「鶏鳴」は「輝かしい将来」を意味します。さらに出世を意味する「功名」と発音が近いので、ますますそのような意味として使われます。雄鶏の傍らに、富の意味を持つ牡丹の花が添えられ、出世し、有名になり、一生裕福になりますようにという祝福に使われる飾りです。

#9-1は、陝西辺りから収集したもので、各種の鳥の図案は、めでたい言葉によく登場するカササギなど縁起のよい鳥です。鳥には手の込んだスプリット・シルク・ステッチが施され、複雑なチェーン・ステッチでできた綺麗な花との組み合わせは、賑やかで生き生きとしています。

#9-2の鳳凰は、伝説上の鳥で、大変美しく、平和と幸福を運んでくれるめでたい鳥として崇められています。歴代の王朝では、皇帝の象徴は龍で、皇后の象徴はこの鳳凰になります。民間にも大変人気が有り、鳳凰にまつわる昔話は豊富に伝えられています。

#9-3は、河南の漢民族の作品で、もう一つのめでたい鳥「綬帯鳥」——三光鳥が登場します。「綬」という字は、寿命の「寿」と同音のため、長生きの象徴の一つになったわけです。また山茶花は、春に咲くということで、三光鳥と組み合わせて、「春光長寿」を意味しています。

Fig . #9-3

花中之舞－**蝴蝶**

蝴蝶因為其美麗輕盈，因此被視為美好吉祥的象徵。戀花的蝴蝶，「蝶戀花」，被拿來比喻甜蜜的愛情和美滿的婚姻。而且「蝶」與「耋」同音，「耋」指九十歲，所以又有長壽的意思。除了漢族常以蝴蝶表示美好之意，蝴蝶在苗族的信仰中也特別重要，因為苗族相信人是從蝶化育而來，故有「蝴蝶媽媽」之稱。

＃10-1的圍兜，採集自貴州的水族自治區，這位年輕的母親在黑色的底布上，挑戰了縝密、複雜度高的馬尾繡，並與鎖繡搭配，一起呈現蝴蝶的美麗與瑰麗的刺繡工藝之美。

「馬尾繡」全名為「馬尾釘線繡」，是水族特有且擅長的技法，在＃10-1這件水族圍兜上，我們可以欣賞到創作者以馬尾毛為線骨，纏以絲線，然後精心地釘縫成長線條、充滿自由奔放之感的圖案，這種緊密的織法，讓作品呈現非凡的立體感，而由馬尾繡層層包圍的是細緻的鎖繡，作者在蝴蝶的身部，採用了飽和的粉紅色與鮮黃、藍色做搭配，加上白色的馬尾繡在蝴蝶兩側的翅膀勾邊，呈現出宛如中國山水畫中「白描」的效果，而在黑色棉布襯托下，這件圍兜益發顯得亮麗。

＃10-2是一只相當漂亮的圍兜，五片的星形加上蝴蝶的紋飾，相當有造型設計感。這件作品以絲為底，上頭的蝴蝶圖案，最引人注意的是以如意雲紋創造出蝴蝶的雙翅，既美麗又洋溢吉慶的祝福。而作者使用正紅、鮮綠、天藍、深紫與銘黃等五色，用在五個星形之上，更將這只圍兜妝點得繽紛斑斕，引人一看再看。

＃10-3的圍兜，採集自廣西三江，以細緻的破絲繡縫製出花朵與十隻蝴蝶，隻隻栩栩如生。作者以金銀線勾邊，並縫製上小小的銅鏡作為裝飾。銅鏡是早期人們喜愛採用的吉祥物，應該和八卦鏡相似，具有避邪的作用。

＃10-4的圍兜造型特殊，除了有五瓣如意雲頭形狀的葉片，還多加了一條長長的劍帶，從圍兜頸項處延伸出來，相當罕見。在五個葉片上，分佈了花朵與蝴蝶的美麗刺繡，豔紅色的花，搭配上鮮藍色展翅飛翔的蝴蝶，顯得既耀眼又美麗。

Fig · #10-1

Fig · #10-2

Fig · #10-3

Dancing Among Flowers—**The Butterfly**

The butterfly can be thought of as the "Chinese Cupid," as well as a bringer of longevity. In the Miao tribal culture, it is believed that mankind is the descendent of the butterfly, so the butterfly is also the mother of all creatures.

In Figure 10-1, the butterflies are depicted in an abstract way, making significant use of negative space, as in Chinese paintings. This is a bib from the Shui tribe, and exemplifies a special technique called horse tail couching stitches.

The bib in Figure 10-2 is stunning. The five panels of contrasting colored silk make up a star shape. The butterflies on the panels recall the curlicues of cloud motifs.

The creator of the bib in Figure 10-3 used little shining metal pieces as mirrors, which are not only items of luck, but also are believed to be a way to ward off evil.

Figure 10-4 shows a unique bib that uses five panels of cloud-like leaves and the addition of a long ribbon. On the five panels, the embroidery is of beautiful flowers and butterflies. The juxtaposition of the reds and blues makes the piece especially enticing to the eye.

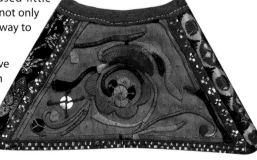

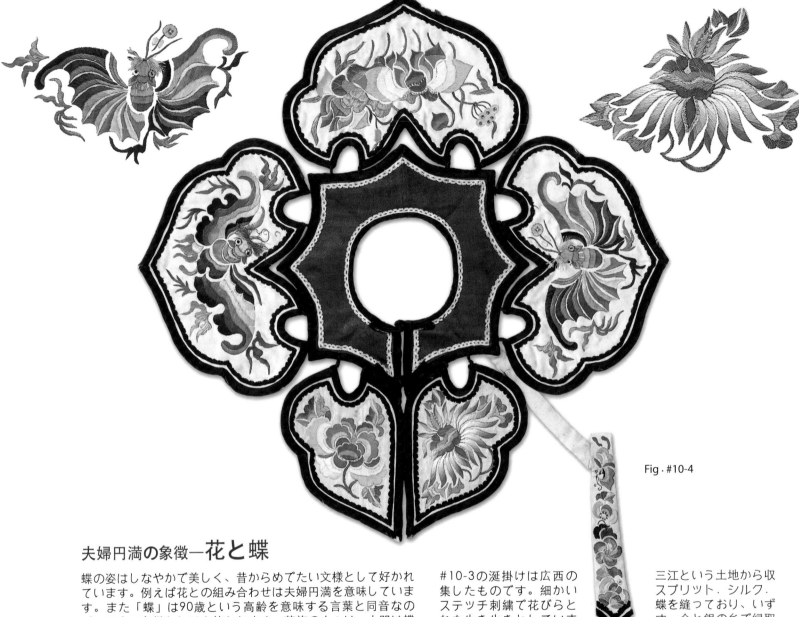

Fig . #10-4

夫婦円満の象徴―花と蝶

蝶の姿はしなやかで美しく、昔からめでたい文様として好かれています。例えば花との組み合わせは夫婦円満を意味しています。また「蝶」は90歳という高齢を意味する言葉と同音なので、長寿の象徴としても使われます。苗族の人々は、人間は蝶より孵化して生まれたと信じ、蝶を大事にしています。

#10-1の涎掛けは、貴州の水族自治区からのものです。黒の生地に、綿密で複雑な技法で刺繍が施され、蝶の美しさと刺繍の洗練さを見せています。

#10-2は、目が醒めるような色鮮やかな涎掛けで、星の形をした5枚の絹の地に、蝶の文様を加えたデザインです。蝶の羽は、雲の形をしためでたい意味を持つ「如意雲紋」からなり、注目に値する傑作です。

#10-3の涎掛けは広西の集したものです。細かいステッチ刺繍で花びらとれも生き生きとしていまりをし、小さな銅鏡を飾た。銅鏡は昔から好かれている縁起物で、魔よけの働きがあると信じられています。

#10-4は、さるのこしかけの形をした4枚の葉の形になっています。首回りのところから伸びている紐に、先の尖がった一本の細い帯がぶら下り、大変珍しいデザインと言えます。赤い花と青い蝶の配色が大変目を惹きます。

三江という土地から収スプリット．シルク．蝶を縫っており、いずす。金と銀の糸で縁取りとして縫いつけまし

小動物

有些圍兜的圖案，繡上多種鳥獸，像＃11-1、＃11-2。＃11-1繡有吉祥的白鶴、梅花鹿，還有綬帶鳥，都是長壽的象徵，還有象徵吉祥的鳳鳥。另外，「猴」與「侯」同音，有「加官封侯」得到福祿之意。猴子性情活潑可愛，特別在《西遊記》中的孫悟空，家喻戶曉，是受人喜愛的角色。

＃11-2是苗族的小孩圍兜。上面有貓頭鷹、老鼠、鳥、蝴蝶和昆蟲，都是人們生活周遭常見的生物。有時刺繡中的昆蟲鳥獸並不具有吉祥如意的意義，母親僅把她所熟悉的事物作為孩兒穿著的裝飾主題，反而顯得親切而自然，也凸顯了苗族媽媽們鮮活靈動的生活創意。

＃11-3是此書中較少見的蠟染作品，上頭繡了花、蝶、鳥、魚，蠟染製造出的反白效果，使得這件幼兒圍兜顯得別有一番風味。

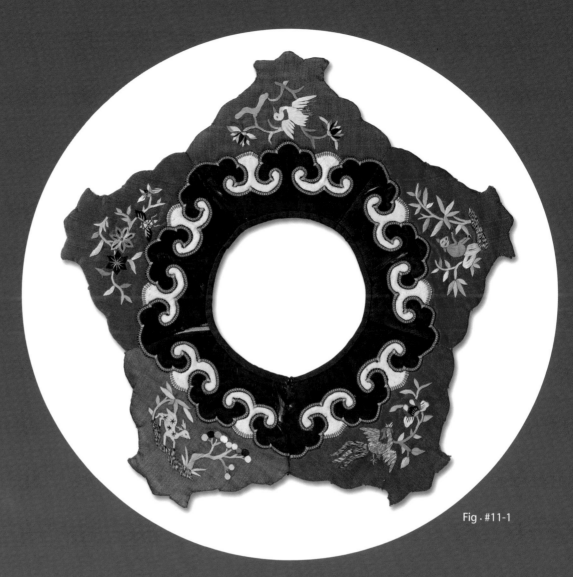

Fig．#11-1

Small Animals—**Birds and Beasts**

Some bibs depict various kinds of birds, such as the ones in Figure 11-1 and Figure 11-2. In Figure 11-1, there is the lucky white crane, the deer, and the long tailed bird—all of which are symbols of longevity. There is also a monkey, which is especially endearing because the monkey plays one of the leading roles in the famed *Tales of the Journey to the West*; the monkey is also well loved for its playfulness.

The bib in Figure 11-2 comes from the Miao people and depicts an owl, a bird, a butterfly, and an insect. These are all creatures from everyday life. At times, the objects or animals a mother chooses to embroider don't necessarily have auspicious significance. They simply stitch what they see, which shows the mother's innocence and keen observation of her immediate surroundings.

In Figure 11-3, we see the batik technique used, which is a rare example in this book. There are flowers, butterflies, and fish, which all have the reverse white effect, due to the batik method.

動物の文様

涎掛けの図案には、色んな動物の文様が見られます。#11-1には、白鶴、鹿、三光鳥などが飾られ、いずれも長寿の象徴です。さらに、蜜蜂、猿なども見られます。猿はといえば、西遊記で大活躍した孫悟空により、庶民に馴染み深い存在になっているほか、猿は中国語で「猴」といい、政府の官職を得て出世するという意味を持つ「侯」と同音のため、縁起のいい動物となりました。

#11-2は、苗族の作品で、ふくろう、鼠、鳥、蝶、昆虫などの文様があり、いずれもよく見かける生き物であります。特にめでたい意味を持っている動物ではなく、日常によく馴染んだ動物を、飾りの主題に登場させていることから、苗族のお母さんの創意工夫が感じられます。

#11-3は、この本では余り見かけないろうけつ染めの技法を採っており、その上に花、蝶、鳥、魚などの刺繍がしてあります。ろうけつ染めによる白抜きの効果は、この作品に特別の味わいを与えています。

Fig . #11-2

Fig . #11-3

第四章

落英繽紛 Chapter 4 Flowers and Plants
第四章 咲き誇る花

⑫

花中之后－牡丹

牡丹是中國傳統名花，雍容華貴，端莊嫵媚，兼具色、香、韻三者之美，是富貴花，也是百花之王。唐朝人稱之「國色天香」，是繁榮昌盛、富貴綿延之象徵。

＃12以紅色為底，將富貴的牡丹花襯托得更加嬌豔華麗，果真是豔麗無比。淡紫色和深紫色的繡線交織，富貴的牡丹也增添了一股少女的嬌羞與浪漫。

Queen of Flowers—**The Peony**

The peony is traditionally a well-known and well-loved flower in Chinese culture. With its regal beauty and elegance, it is known as the flower of wealth, as well as the king of all flowers.

The lavender and dark purple peonies in Figure 12 are romantic and that much more striking because of their contrast with the red background. This is an especially feminine.

花の女王—牡丹

牡丹は中国では昔から大変知られている花です。その姿は富貴にして端正で、色、香り、風情の三つの美を備えた花の女王であります。唐の時代の人々は、牡丹を繁栄と富貴の象徴として愛していました。#12は、赤の生地に牡丹の花を添え、その艶やかな姿は比類の無いものです。また花びらは薄紫と深い紫の配色により、少女のような若々しい風情も感じられます。

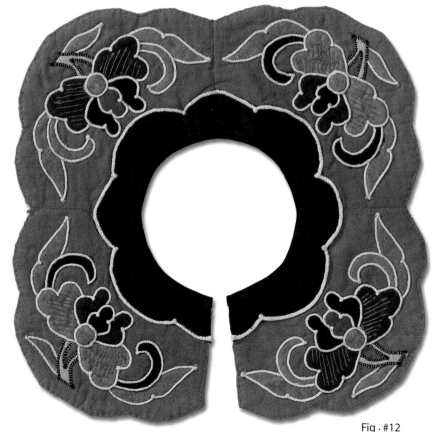

Fig . #12

⑬

冰霜鐵骨─梅花

＃13的圍兜上繡的是冰霜鐵骨的梅花，中國的文人向
來對梅花情有獨鍾，曲折的枝椏在寒冷的冬夜裡傲
然挺立，常被引伸為文人的一身傲骨，而她淡
雅的清香隨著微風飄送，也被形容為「暗
香」，是很有文人味的花朵。年輕的母親
用淡雅的梅花為孩兒縫製圍兜，也透
露了希望孩兒日後具有文采的期望。
這只圍兜採用了貼布的手法來表
現，細細欣賞玩味，似乎梅花的
暗香也隱隱撲鼻而來了呢！

Plum Blossom

Chinese scholars and writers
have long had a love affair
with the plum blossom.
The contrast between its
scraggly branches and
small delicate blossoms
is quite poetic, as well
as its resilience in the
harsh winters. The plum
blossom is a very "literary"
flower. When a mother has
embroidered a bib with
plum blossoms, like the one
in Figure 13, it shows that she
may be hoping that her baby
will grow up to have talent in the
literary arts.

厳寒に屈しない冬の梅

＃13は梅の文様です。中国の文人は、梅に
対して特別な思い入れがあります。梅の木の
枝が冷たい夜に毅然と立っている姿は、文人の決
して屈することのない気骨に喩えられ、またその清
らかな香りまで、文人の淡白な姿を思わせています。雅
やかな梅の文様をあしらうことによって、わが子も文才に恵ま
れますようにという母親の願いが伺えます。

Fig.＃13

四季平安

＃14這是以四季花卉養在盆（瓶）中為主題，以「瓶」與「平」同音，稱之為「四季平（瓶）安」。這件圍兜採集自浙江一帶，十個葉片造型相當華麗，也可歸類為小型的霞被。圍兜上的花卉與瓶子，以十字繡來表現，顯得既細緻又工整，四種顏色調配，從橘、桃紅、黃到綠色，斑斕的色彩搭配起來卻毫不俗氣，反而使得這只圍兜顯得格外地華美與富貴。

日々無事を祈る—四季平安

＃14は、盆や瓶の中に植えたり挿したりする四季の花々をテーマにしました。「瓶」は平安の「平」と同音のため、このような図案は「四季平安」という縁起のよい名前を持っています。この涎掛けは浙江辺りから収集したもので、10枚の葉の形は非常に華やかで、肩掛けにもなります。クロスステッチの技法を使い、橙色、桃色、黄色から緑色まで、大変多彩だが、気品のある作品です。

Peace for All Seasons—**The Four Seasons**

Because the pronunciation of "vase" (*ping*) and "peace" (*ping an*) are the same in Chinese, the depiction of a vase—especially when it involves flowers from all four seasons—symbolizes perpetual peace. Cross stitches are used in the embroidery of the bib in Figure 14.

Fig · #14

百花齊放

#15以美麗的花朵圖案和貼布技巧縫製而成。在中國民間的刺繡藝術裡，有所謂的「百家衣」，縫製衣裳的婦女到鄰近各家要布，將各家布料裁剪之後，重新拼貼縫製成新的衣裳，給家中小孩穿戴。民間相信：家中孩童穿戴這種百家衣之後會長的特別好，而以這只圍兜來看，一片花團錦簇，也的確顯得特別喜氣。

咲き誇る花

#15の美しい花の図案は、アップリケの技法で作られています。民間の刺繍芸術の中に、「百家衣」というのがあり、母親たちが他の家々から布切れを集め、縫い繋いで、自分の子供に作った衣装です。この「百家衣」を着れば我が子は無事育つと人々は信じていました。色々な花が賑やかに咲き、ほのぼのとした雰囲気が感じられます。

All Flowers Are In Bloom

The bib in Figure 15 is made with appliqués of many different flowers and is meant to give the impression that there are hundreds upon hundreds of flowers sewn on. There is a type of clothing in Chinese folk art called the "hundred patches cloth." The mother will go around to all the neighbors in her village and ask for scraps of fabric. She will then sew the scraps together to create one new shirt for her child—rather like a quilt. This "hundred patches cloth" is meant to bring the child good luck. In the same way, the abundance of flowers sewn from different patches of scraps on this bib, along with its appliqué technique, make it look like it was meant to serve the same purpose.

Fig‧#15

Fig · #16-1

⑯ 瓜瓞綿綿

大曰瓜，小曰瓞，「瓜瓞綿綿」在《詩經大雅》就有出現：「綿綿瓜瓞，民之初生，自土沮漆。」指瓜之正本初生者小，其蔓不絕，至末而後大。本意是歌頌周朝像瓜瓞一樣，子孫眾多，代代相續。

＃16-1，繡有十二個金瓜，金瓜即一般所俗稱的南瓜，豐潤的果實和金黃的色澤帶來吉祥富貴的意味。古時以三、九兩個數字代表多數，這只圍兜上一口氣繡了十二個南瓜，每三個為一叢，叢叢相連，象徵帶來多子多孫，瓜瓞綿綿，富貴也連連的的吉慶之兆。

＃16-2為採集自安徽一帶的圍兜，這只圍兜以珍貴的白鍛為底布，應該是富貴人家的幼兒用品，並以特別的別絨技法一針一線

縫製而成，相當精細美麗。圍兜上繡有蝴蝶和各式瓜果，如荔枝、石榴與桃子，並有金線穿插其中，顯得精緻而富貴。

桃，向來是長壽的象徵，中國神話中傳說西王母的花園種了仙桃樹，三千年一開花，三千年一結果，吃了仙桃可以增壽六百年。西王母在收成時，依例會舉辦「仙桃宴」，邀請眾家神仙為嘉賓。

＃16-3上繡有佛手。佛手，又名佛手柑，成熟時帶有濃厚的香氣，因為果實前端裂開分散有如手指，而果實基部呈圓形狀的手掌，故稱「佛手」，因其香氣濃厚，被拿來供佛，也由於其與佛的關係，因此認為佛手能給人帶來平安。這只圍兜以金線繡邊，判斷可能也是有錢人家的圍兜。

To Have Many Descendants—**Melons**

In Figure 16-1, there are many "golden melons," or pumpkins, on the bib, which means that this mother is hoping for a big family with many future grandchildren.

In Figure 16-2, in addition to butterflies and melons, the peach has long been the symbol of longevity. In Chinese fairytale, Xi Wang Mu, the Royal Lady of the West, lived in a palace surrounded by beautiful fairy peach trees. These fairy peaches ripened only once every three thousand years and whoever ate one would live for six hundred years.

Because the bib in Figure 16-2 uses luxurious white silk satin as background, it is safe to assume that it came from a wealthy family. On the bib we see a butterfly, along with peaches, lychees, and pomegranates—all luxurious fruits that symbolize life and longevity.

The fruit in Figure 16-3 is a citrus fruit that gives off an intense fragrance. Because of its finger-like shape, it is referred to as Buddha's hand and brings peace. The Buddha's hand also denotes wealth because it captures the gesture of the hand clasping money.

Fig · #16-2

Fig · #16-3

子孫繁栄を願う瓜の文様

瓜類は自分が孕んだ種だけで、沢山の瓜を新たに生むことができるので、子孫繁栄の縁起物として人気があります。#16-1は、3つずつ生えている南瓜(かぼちゃ)の図案が計12個刺繍されています。南瓜は綺麗な金色をしていて、中国人が見て大変めでたい感じがするものです。またどうして3つかというと、昔の人にとって3や9という数字は「多数」という意味もありました。この図柄は3つずつ互いに繋がっているので、子孫繁栄と喜びの意味を合わせ持っています

#16-2は安徽の辺りで収集したもので、高価な白緞子を生地にしていることから、お金持ちの家の物と思われます。蝶やライチ、石榴、桃など、各種の果物の刺繍文様と金糸の色が映え、大変豪華な感じがする作品です。

#16-3には左上に「仏の手」という文様が見られます。「仏の手」とはとても香りがよい柑橘類の果物で、果実の先の方が分かれていて指のように見え、また後の方は人間の手のひらの様に見えます。その形から、「仏の手」という名前を得ました。人々は縁起物としてよくお釈迦さまにお供えします。

葫蘆

葫蘆藤蔓綿延，結實累累，籽粒繁多，被視為多子多孫的象徵。葫蘆蔓之「蔓」與「萬」諧音，寓意萬代綿長。同時，古代神話中認為葫蘆是天地的縮影和象徵，裡面充滿著靈氣。民間也將葫蘆當成一種避邪鎮妖之物，八仙之一的鐵拐李手裡就拿著葫蘆。

＃17-1的圍兜，整件就是一個葫蘆形，是圍兜裡相當特殊而罕見的造型，相信即取自葫蘆多子多孫的吉慶之意。

值得欣賞的是這件圍兜上還縫上一只口袋，上面印有廣告詞的字樣，顯然是這塊布料的廣告，縫製這只圍兜的母親，不知從哪裡取來此塊布料，就乾脆縫在自家孩兒的衣服上，取自生活，用於生活的態度，顯得怡然而自得。葫蘆下方繡有一隻貓和蝴蝶，即「耄耋」（貓蝶），希望帶給孩兒長壽吉祥。

＃17-2為中國北方的圍兜作品，以五個葫蘆圍成圓形，取多子多孫多富貴之意，鮮豔的色塊以貼布手法呈現，具有天真浪漫的童趣。

Hu-Lu—**The Gourd**

The hourglass-shaped gourd (*hu-lu*) symbolizes longevity and many births. In Chinese fairytale, the gourd is also a symbol of heaven and earth, so it is considered to be filled with spirituality and has the ability to ward off evil.

The bib in Figure 17-1 is in the shape of a gourd—a very rare and unique design in this collection of bibs. The curious detail about this bib is that it uses fabric upon which is printed an advertisement for that same fabric. The mother must have used whatever fabric she had around the house to make it into a bib for her child—very practical and creative, indeed! On the bottom portion of the gourd there is a butterfly and a kitten, meant to bring the child fortune and longevity.

Figure 17-2 is from northern China: using the appliqué technique, five gourds are grouped into a round circle. The color arrangement gives off a gay and naive mood.

子沢山の瓢箪

瓢箪も沢山の種を持っているので、子孫繁栄の象徴として親しまれています。また瓢箪のつる「蔓」は、「萬」と同音なため、代々終わることなく、延々と延びるという意味も持っています。#17-1の涎掛けは、全体に瓢箪の形をしており、大変珍しいものです。注目するべきところは、袋が付いていて、広告らしい言葉がその上に印刷されています。何処かで手に入れた布の切れに、たまたま広告が印刷してあり、母親は構わずにそのまま使ったということが想像できます。瓢箪の下に蝶と猫があり、この組み合わせは典型的な長寿を願う文様です。

#17-2は中国北方のもので、5つの瓢箪に囲まれ円形になったもので、子孫繁栄の願いが込められ、実に天真爛漫で可愛らしい作品です。

Fig . #17-1

Fig . #17-2

連中三元

#18的圍兜上，可以見到荔枝、桂圓和核桃，都屬圓形的果實。三種果實圓圓地畫在一起，寓「連中三元」，即奪得舊時科舉考試中鄉試、會試、殿試的第一名。這件圍兜除了有吉慶的果實外，在圍兜六個葉片的尖端又呈現石榴的造型，流露母親對孩兒滿滿的祝福。

試験合格─連中三元

#18には、ライチ、龍眼、胡桃など、丸い形の果実が登場します。中国語の「丸い」─「圓」は、「首席」を意味する「元」と同音のため、丸い果実が3つ丸く並んでいるということは、3段階ある中国にある出世のための「科挙試験」に、全て合格することを意味しています。

The Three Accomplishments

On the bib in Figure 18, there are lychees, walnuts, and other fruits that are all round in shape. "Round" is pronounced *yuan*; and in feudal China, the number one candidate for the civil service examination in the county test is called *Jie Yuan*, the winner of the provincial test is called *Huei Yuan*, and the final winner in the imperial examination is called *Zhuang Yuan*. So if one gets three numbers successively, it is called *San Yuan* (three Yuan). Mothers use the three round-shaped fruits to give the symbolic wishes for her child to have the San Yuan.

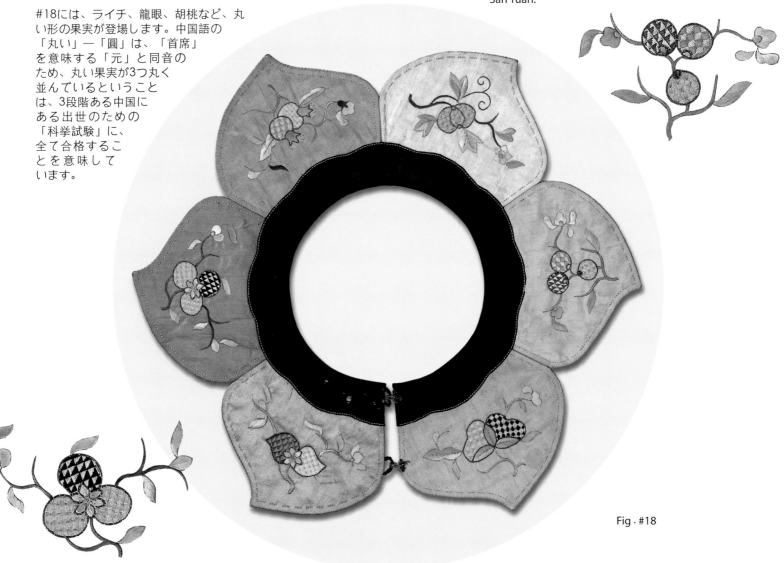

Fig . #18

民間故事與神話 Chapter 5　Folk Tales and Fairytales
第伍章　民間昔話と神話

⑲

西遊記

如果問小孩子最熟悉的民間故事是什麼？答案可能就是＃19這只圍兜上所描繪的故事《西遊記》了。

《西遊記》是明朝吳承恩所寫的神魔小說，敘述唐僧三藏赴西天取經，其弟子孫悟空在路上降服妖魔，排除險阻的事蹟。另外兩個徒弟是沙悟淨和豬八戒。這部小說的人物生動，情節曲折，是家喻戶曉的民間故事。

這只收集自山東的圍兜，有了西遊記故事的烘托，顯得格外有趣和引人入勝，當媽媽跟小孩講《西遊記》的故事，一邊也把西遊記中的人物全繡在圍兜上，這是何等的親切與傳神，也可見媽媽的想像力有多麼豐富。

Fig.#19

Journey to the West

If you ask Chinese children which folktale they are most familiar with, it would most likely be the tale that is depicted in Figure 19—*Journey to the West*.

Journey to the West is a novel from the Ming dynasty describing the journey that Monk San Tsang (Tang Dynasty) and his three disciples take to the west, in search of a holy Buddhist sutra. One of the disciples is Sun Wu Kong, the mischievous monkey who gets into all kinds of trouble. The other two disciples are Sha Wu Jing, the water goblin, and Zhu Ba Jie, the pig. This novel is filled with interesting characters, adventure, and excitement and is popular among younger children.

This bib depicts the four main characters of the novel. One can easily imagine the mother pointing to the characters on this bib as she tells her child the stories from *Journey to the West*.

西遊記

中国の子供たちに一番よく知っている昔話は何と聞いたら、間違いなく「西遊記」と答えることでしょう。#19は、まさにこの西遊記の場面です。この涎掛けは山東から収集してきた作品で、西遊記に出てくる人物が文様となり、一層面白くなっています。わが子に西遊記の話をしながら、一針一針その人物たちを布に刺繍していく、幸せに満ちたお母さんの姿が、眼に浮かびます。

Fig · #20

A Hero Raised by Nature

The bib in Figure 20 tells of a Shantung folk tale. The story goes like this: A female dragon once gave birth to a human baby and then abandoned it in the wild. After happening upon this baby, a tiger decides to feed the baby with its own milk. Meanwhile, an eagle swoops in to help build shelter for the baby. This baby then grows up to be Hsiang Yu, the King of Chu who eventually overthrows the Qin Dynasty.

On this bib, you can see the naked baby having just been born, the female dragon on the right, the eagle in the middle, and the tiger on the left.

虎と鷹に守られた龍の子の話

#20は山東から収集した涎掛けで、昔話に基づいたものです。龍が生んだ赤ん坊は野原に捨てられ、虎に拾われました。虎が自分の乳で育っているところへ、鷹が飛んできて赤ん坊を暑い陽射しから守るために、日覆いを建ててくれたという話です。なお、この赤ん坊はのちに秦国を屈服させた楚国の王—項羽だと伝えられています。

この涎掛けには、物語に出てくる裸の赤ん坊が中央にいて、周りに橙色の龍、灰色の鷹、桃色の虎が守るように囲んでいます。涎掛けを手に、我が子に話を聞かせる母と、夢中に聞いている子の姿が眼に浮かんできそうです。

(20)

龍生，虎奶，雕打棚

#20這只圍兜上的圖案，取材自山東的民間故事－「龍生，虎奶，雕打棚」，這個故事也常在剪紙作品中出現。故事是說，有一個人為龍女所生，生下來後被丟在野外，後來有老虎發現了這個嬰兒，便親自哺奶餵養，又有老鷹飛來為他搭建棚子，以免被炎熱的陽光灼傷。傳說中，這個孩子便是楚霸王項羽。

在這只圍兜的面上，可以看到裸身的嬰兒被生下來，右邊有橘色龍鱗的是生他的龍女，中間灰色的是大老鷹，而在左邊有一隻粉紅色的老虎，非常地生動、可愛。

寶寶聽媽媽講述這個故事時，一定聽得興味盎然。

虎松打虎

#21是收集自中國北方的圍兜，圍兜面上繡著一個男人在打拳，旁邊有一隻老虎，推測可能是在民間廣為流傳的《武松打虎》故事。媽媽們有時候會把熟悉的民間故事一併繡在孩兒的圍兜上。

《武松打虎》是中國著名的小說《水滸傳》中的一段故事，描述英勇的武松在景陽岡上徒手制服凶猛老虎的故事，透露出縫製這只圍兜的母親，希望孩兒長大之後能夠擁有武松般的機智與過人膽識。另外，在圍兜面上還繡有喜鵲與梅枝，以及「耄（貓）耋（蝴蝶）富貴」等圖案，旁邊的佛手與小孩，可能是從「瓜瓞綿綿」延伸而來。

Wu Song Kills the Tiger

Mothers will often embroider familiar folk tales and fairy tales onto their baby's bibs. This one in Figure 21 is a story from the famous Chinese novel, *All Men Are Brothers*, about how a hero named Wu Song kills a deadly tiger. It is easy to imagine that this mother hoped that her baby would inherit Wu Song's courage and strength.

武松の虎退治

#21は中国北方地方のもので、拳術のポーズをしている男の人の側に、虎が一匹佇んでいます。昔話でよく知られている「武松の虎退治」の話に基づいた文様ではないかと推測されます。自分の熟知する昔話を、わが子の着るものに縫い込むことが時々見られます。この虎退治の文様は、わが子にも武松のような機智と勇気を持つように、という母親の願いが込められているようです。さらにカササギと梅、猫と蝶、仏の手と子供などの組み合わせは、いずれもよく知られるめでたい文様です。

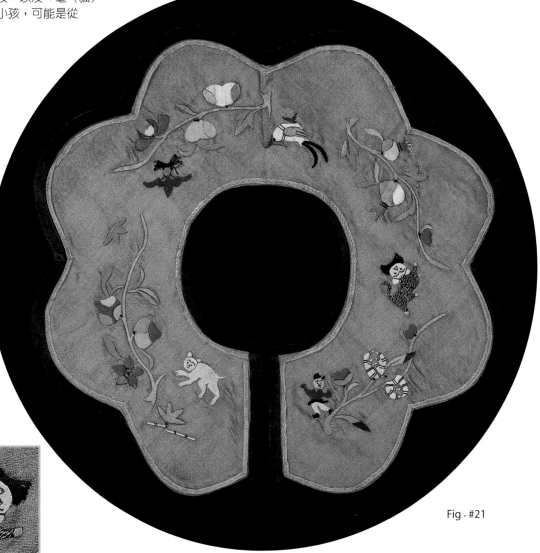

Fig・#21

苗族神話

這裡介紹一系列有關苗族神話的圍兜。這些圍兜都是貴州凱里翁項的苗族作品。苗族內流傳許多有關他們祖先的故事，經過代代口耳相傳，婦女們將這些故事繡在服飾上，讓下一代的孩童也能瞭解祖先的由來，是極具傳承意義的常民藝術。

這三個作品中，＃22-2打籽繡作品可能是較早的作品，三只圍兜都是描述苗族祖先央公央妹的故事，充滿天馬行空的想像力，小朋友多在節慶時穿戴上作為裝飾。

＃22-1描繪的是央妹坐在轎子上，由十二生肖抬她進山洞。仔細欣賞，圍兜面上有央公抽煙斗、喝茶，猴乘羊，以及雙頭龍等圖案，濃厚的神話色彩，相當有趣，繡工也非常精緻。

＃22-2以特殊的打籽繡技法來呈現苗族的神話故事，上面可以見到苗族祖先央公央妹的圖騰，還有公雞、蝴蝶以及猴子為人撐傘的畫面。而以粉紅色及綠色為主的繡線，搭配上穩重的黑底，兩相輝映，顯得相當突出。

＃22-3繡工繁複華麗，這只圍兜是貴州施洞的作品，上頭繡有各式人面鳥身的獸類，洋溢苗族獨特的神秘色彩。

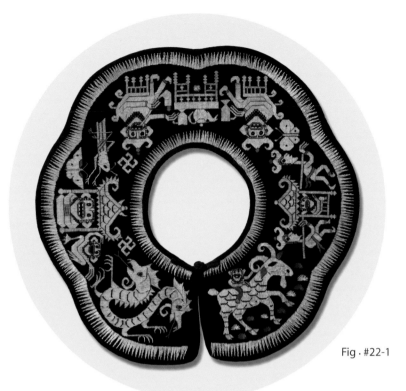

Fig · #22-1

Fairytales from the Miao Tribe

This is a series of bibs from Miao tribes in the Guei Zhou area. Within the Miao tribe, there has always been a great circulation of creation myths and myths about their ancestors. These oral "histories" were often the subject of needlework because mothers wanted to pass on these stories to the next generation.

In Figure 22-1, we see a bib that has a lot going on. The twelve animals of the zodiac are carrying Iang Mei—ancestor of the Miao people—on a sedan chair. Upon close examination, we can see creatures smoking pipes, a monkey riding a goat, a double-headed dragon, and more. All of these images are full of fantastical imagination and other-worldly beings.

In Figure 22-2 and Figure 22-3, we see the same creature that has

 a human head and a bird's body. This kind of deification (half man, half bird or half man, half beast) can be seen in Miao minority people and other ancient cultures.

Fig · #22-2

第壹部 幼兒的第一件衣裳—圍兜

苗族の神話

苗族の神話にまつわる一連の涎掛けをご紹介します。いずれも貴州の凱里翁項という地方から収集した苗族作品です。

苗族は、祖先に関する昔話を口で伝えると共に、それらの物語を子供服に刺繍し記録しておくという、極めて有意義な習慣があります。

#22の1-3の作品は、比較的に初期の作品であります。3枚の涎掛けとも苗族の祖先である「央公央妹」の話に関わるものです。神話好きな苗族の母親が、神秘的でユーモアたっぷりの文様を、素晴らしい想像力によって上手く表現しています。これらの涎掛けは、いずれも祭りの際に子供たちが飾りとして身に付けるものです。

Fig . #22-3

暗八仙／暗八寶

古代傳說中八仙的執器物所組成的一種吉祥圖案，稱之為
「暗八仙」。包括漢鐘離所執的葵扇，據說有起死回生
的法力；呂洞賓所執的寶劍，可以驅魔；鐵拐李手執
葫蘆，代表不朽不滅的友誼；張果老手持魚鼓，
具有占卜的能力；曹國舅手持的拍版，可以聽
到天堂的天籟；何仙姑手捧荷花，代表和睦恩
愛君子花，比喻人修身不染；韓湘子手拿管
簫，具有妙音入身，健康長壽的用意；而
藍采和手提花藍，具有非凡的神通力。

此外，所謂「暗八寶」，包含：方勝，
繼續不斷之意；磬，同「慶」；犀角
杯，代表隆盛；艾葉，代表高貴；寶
珠，代表熱情光明；金錢，代表富貴；
菱鏡，代表美；書，代表智慧。

＃23這件收集自安徽、山西一帶的圍
兜，上頭即繡有吉祥的暗八仙與佛教的
暗八寶，並製成色彩斑爛的百家衣，這
件圍兜年代應該相當久遠，但顏色仍然
保持著當初的鮮豔美麗，難能可貴。

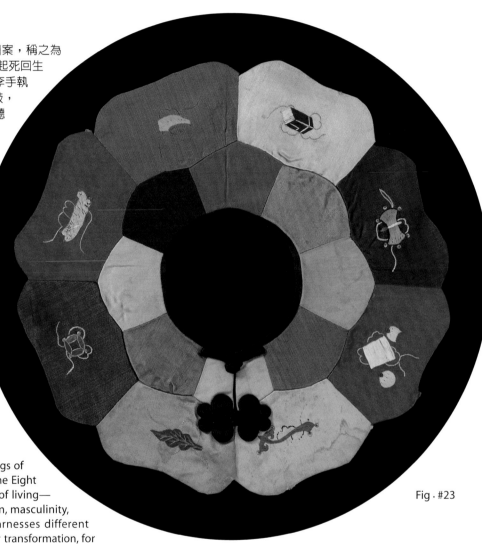

Fig . #23

Eight Immortals' Eight Treasures

The Eight Immortals (*Ba Xian*) are legendary beings of
Taoism that are often depicted in embroidery. The Eight
Immortals each represent a different condition of living—
wealth, poverty, youth, age, aristocracy, plebeian, masculinity,
and femininity. Each of the immortals also harnesses different
supernatural powers—immortality, invisibility, or transformation, for
example.

The Eight Treasures are represented by various antique symbols on
embroidery and are represented by various categories—they may
be the various emblems of the Eight Immortals, The Eight Precious
Organs of the Buddha's Body, or the Eight Auspicious Signs. The Eight
Auspicious Signs include the pearl (passion and brightness); lozenge
(infinity); stone chime (festivity); rhinoceros' horns (happiness); coin
(wealth); mirror (beauty); book (wisdom); and leaf (elegance).

The bib in Figure 23 depicts objects from the Eight Treasures, all of
which are meant to bring the baby good fortune.

仏教の宝物—八宝

八宝は仏教の法器で、それぞれ知恵、光明、富貴、美麗、隆盛
などのめでたい意味を持っています。この涎掛けは豊富な色彩
で「百家衣」に仕上げられています。相当な年代を経ていると
思われますが、色彩は今尚新しい時の様な鮮やかさを保ってい
て、大変得難いものです。

童玩世界　Chapter 6　Children's World of Playing

㉔

嬰戲圖之——**童子玩爆竹**

孩兒玩耍或在生活中的各種活動，在成人的眼光中是天真無邪、開心快樂的象徵，因此，嬰戲圖也是屬於吉祥如意的圖案。

例如：童子玩爆竹是過年時的遊戲。傳說中「年」是可怕的山鬼，到村子裡來專吃小孩，帶來疾病，於是村民以火燃竹，畢剝有聲，稱之為爆竹，用以驅鬼。南朝古書有記載：「正月一日雞鳴而起，先庭前爆竹，心辟山燥惡鬼」，後來的人以紙捲火藥，點燃發聲，也稱爆竹，或叫爆仗，有「爆竹一聲除舊，桃符萬象更新」，即除舊佈新，以及報平安的意思。

#24的圍兜採集自安徽民間，面上繡有非常精彩多樣的嬰戲圖。七個葉片上繡有七種不同的嬰戲圖案，有放鞭炮、舞鞭、蹴鞠（即踢毽子）、玩撥浪鼓、抓蜻蜓、打拳、追逐蝴蝶戲耍，每一幅都值得細細欣賞。看七個童子睜大了眼，手舞足蹈，玩得投入又盡興，彷彿也讓人沾染了一身孩童的天真浪漫。

另外，這只圍兜採用纏金的技法，每一葉片並設計成如意雲鎖的形狀，顯得更加特別、更加吉祥。

Children Setting Off Firecrackers

To a parent's eye, the image of children playing is also an image of innocence and purity. Therefore, embroidery of scenes of children playing is considered auspicious.

According to folklore, the *nian* (the character for "year") was a frightening mountain beast who would come into villages to taunt and eat little children, bring disease, and set the village on fire. Therefore, every new year, children would set off firecrackers to shoo away the *nian*. Scenes of children playing with firecrackers are often embroidered.

In Figure 24, on the seven petals of the bib, we can see children engaged in all sorts of activity—playing with firecrackers, chasing butterflies, performing martial arts, and catching dragonflies, to name a few. Every panel is a feast for the eyes. All the children are depicted with large, excited eyes, and their movement lets the viewer feel the innocence and happiness of childhood.

嬰戯図その1—爆竹で遊ぶ子供たち

子供が遊んでいる場面は、いつ見ても楽しいものです。「嬰戯図」という幼児が戯れている場面は、中国ではめでたい文様になります。例えば子供の爆竹遊びは、中国のお正月の定番です。お正月を新年と言いますが、言い伝えによると、「年」とは山から下りてきた恐ろしい鬼のことで、子供を食べたり、病気を持ってきたりするので、村人は竹を焼いて、破裂音を出して威嚇し、鬼を退散させたというのが爆竹の始まりだそうです。

#24は、安徽という地方から来たもので、色鮮やかな「嬰戯図」が飾られています。7枚の葉にそれぞれ爆竹遊び、鞭遊び、羽根蹴り、でんでん太鼓遊び、トンボ捕り、蝶捕り、体操など、7つの異なった嬰戯図が刺繍されています。どれもじっくりと鑑賞するに値し、見る人の童心を呼び起すような傑作です。また金糸で縁取りをした上、葉の形が「如意雲」（さるのこしかけの形をした雲、縁起物）の形なので、めでたい意味が一層感じ取られます。

Fig . #24

Fig . #25

㉕

嬰戲圖之二－**吹簫玩扇**

＃25的圍兜也是安徽民間的作品，似乎是給女孩使用的圍兜，因此這只圍兜上面繡的七個嬰戲圖案，也都是模樣可愛的女娃兒，分別進行吹簫、拿扇、吊金錢等各式遊戲活動，此外加上蓮花的圖案，寓有「蓮花生子」的意涵。這只圍兜採用盤金、緞帶勾邊，加上七個葉片豐富的色彩，顯出女孩特有的美麗嬌豔。

Girls Playing with Flute and Fan

The bib in Figure 25 was most likely made for a girl because the seven petals that form the bib each show a young girl engaged in various activities—playing the flute, holding a fan, catching butterflies, etc. The lotus flowers included in each panel also make the bib especially feminine.

嬰戯図その2―**笛や扇子で遊ぶ子供たち**

＃25も安徽から来たもので、女の子用ではないかと思われます。なぜなら登場する子供は全員女の子だからです。それぞれ笛を吹いたり、扇子で遊んでいたりしています。また蓮の花（蓮は子孫繁栄の意味を持っている）が飾られています。この色鮮やかな涎掛けには、綺麗な縁取りや精緻な細工で、女の子の持ち物ならではの華やかさが感じ取られます。

26

嬰戲圖之三─**童子執蓮花**

＃26圍兜上，有個梳著雙髻的女娃兒雙手舉花，也是屬於嬰戲圖的一種變化，稱為「童子執蓮花」。作者使用貼布手法來表現花的層疊效果，與藤蔓的美麗曲線，加上紅色的主色，顯得喜氣洋洋，很適合年節氣氛。

嬰戲図その3─**蓮の花を持つ子供**

＃26では、髪の毛を両耳の所で束ねている女の子が、両手に花を持っています。これも嬰戲図から生まれた文様の一つです。アップリケの技法により、花びらが重なっている様子を上手く表現しています。また蔓の美しいラインは、変化のある赤い色で合わせて、新年に相応しい楽しい文様となっています。

Child Holding Lotus

In Figure 26, a female child with braided hair is holding a lotus flower in each hand. This image is said to represent fertility for northern Chinese. Here, the appliqué technique is used. The bold use of red and black make this an especially striking piece.

Fig · #26

Fig · #27

㉗

嬰戲圖之四 – 福壽無疆

#27整件圍兜是由桃子形狀的葉片，圍著一個赤裸身體的小娃娃。小娃娃手上舉花，肚子上開了個洞，正好作為圍兜的頸項開口。身旁繡有頂端開了花的「壽」字，以期盼小娃兒順利長大，長壽富貴。

嬰戯図その4—永遠の幸福と長寿

#27は桃の形をしている一枚の葉で、真ん中に裸の赤ん坊が大きく描かれています。赤ん坊は両手に花を持っていて、体の両側に「寿」という字があり、すくすくと大きく育ち、幸せに長生きできますようにという親の願いが込められています。

May One Attain Boundless Happiness and Longevity

The shape of the bib in Figure 27 is that of a peach. There is a naked baby filling the entire bib, with a hole in its stomach where the actual baby's neck would be. The character for longevity appears on either side of the bib, wishing the baby a long and healthy life.

㉘

吉慶連續紋

如果一個吉慶符號，代表一個祝福；那麼把一個個不同的吉慶符號串連在一起，細細一針一線地繡在衣裳上，那是代表多麼深長和綿延的情感啊！＃28的圍兜，綴滿了美麗的吉慶連續紋，可以慢慢欣賞。

這裡的吉慶連續紋，包括了八角花紋、萬字紋（卍）和盤長，其中，八角花紋是由太陽紋衍生而來，這種成輻射狀的圖案，不僅年代久遠而且許多民族都看的到，可能是源自對太陽的崇拜。

萬字圖紋，在古代印度、波斯、希臘等國家被視為太陽或火的象徵，後來用在佛教釋迦牟尼佛胸部的印記，在中國是萬德吉祥的意思。萬字紋有向左旋和向右旋兩種形式，兩者均通用。此符號在武則天時代（約七世紀）制訂此符號的讀法為「萬」沿用至今。

盤長是佛教中的八寶（亦稱「八吉祥」）之一。盤長有「四環貫徹，一切通明」之意，象徵連綿不斷之意，在中國結藝術中，也常可見到這種吉慶的盤長結。

めでたい連続紋

異なる種類のめでたい祝福の記号を繋げ合わせて、一針一針衣装に縫い付ければ、どんなに深くて長い祝福になるのでしょう。#28の涎掛けは、そのような発想の元で生まれた美しい連続紋にびっしりと埋められています。時間を掛けてゆっくりと楽しみたいものです。

文様として、卍(萬)字紋、盤長結び紋、太陽の文様から生まれた八角紋などがあります。

輻射状の八角紋は、中国の多くの民族が共用しているもので、歴史も長く、太陽に対する崇拝から来たのではないかと思われます。

また、中国語で「萬」と発音する「卍」字紋は、古代インド、ペルシア、ギリシャなどの国では、太陽や火のシンボルとされていました。またお釈迦様の胸にある印としても使われました。中国では「萬德吉祥」というめでたい意味を持っています。なお、万字「卍」は鉤の方向が反対の右万字でも、万字と読み意味も同じです。

「盤長」は仏教の八つの宝物の一つで、「長く続き永遠に絶えない」ことを意味しています。中国の縄結び芸術の中でもよく登場します。

Continuous Auspicious Symbols

If one auspicious symbol represents one wish, then a series of interconnected symbols would represent a hopefulness that runs very deep! The bib in Figure 28 shows just such a bib, filled with symbols of good fortune, wealth and success, including the swastika (regarded as the seal of the Buddhist heart, or as a sign of the sun); the lozenge (one of the eight treasures, which symbolizes infinity); the mystic knot (continuity); and the eight radiant floral patterns, which symbolize the worship of the sun.

Fig・#28

29

八卦

八卦是古書周易中，用以論述萬物變化的基本圖形。「—」象徵陽，「--」代表陰。八卦中的乾（☰）代表天，坤（☷）代表地，震（☳）代表雷，巽（☴）代表風，坎（☵）代表水，离（☲）代表火，艮（☶）代表山，兌（☱）代表澤，以這八種自然現象推測自然和社會的變化，並認為陰陽兩種勢力的相互作用是產生萬物的根源。太極（陰陽）和八卦在道家認為有神通廣大，震懾邪惡的威力。

#29-1圍兜的八個葉片上，在環繞頸項的圓形開口邊上即繡有八卦紋，代表萬物生生不絕。此外，縫製這只圍兜的媽也親手繡上佛手、蝴蝶和如意雲紋，希望帶給寶寶綿長的福氣。 #29-2則在八個花瓣狀的圓弧布面上，繡以八卦圖形，為孩兒祈福。

Fig . #29-1

The Ba-Gua—**The Eight Trigrams**

The Eight Diagrams are various combinations of lines arranged in a circle, which symbolizes the evolution of nature and its cyclical changes. The Eight Trigrams are the series of lines from which the vital elements of the universe were created. The Eight Trigrams are drawn with two symbols, represented by a continuous straight line (—) called Yang (the symbol of male principle) and a broken line (--) called Ying (the symbol of the female principle.) The Eight Trigrams are considered to have the power of protecting children from misfortune.

On each of the eight petals that form the bib in Figure 29-1, the Eight Trigrams are stitched and represent the unending cycle of life. The mother has also added other auspicious symbols here, such as the Buddha's hand, a butterfly, and cloud motifs. Figure 29-2 is a simpler and more direct representation of the Eight Trigrams on a bib.

宇宙万物の変化を論ずる際の基本図形—八卦

八卦は、中国の古い文書「周易」の中で、宇宙万物の変化を論ずる際の基本図形とされていました。例えば陽、陰、天、地、雷、風、水、火、山、沢など、それぞれを代表する図形があります。この八つの自然現象によって、大自然と社会の変化を推測することが出来ると考えられています。また、陰と陽の二つの力の相互作用によって、万物が生まれるという考え方も持っています。ちなみに中国の道教では、八卦と太極は邪悪なものを押さえる強いパワーを持っていると信じられています。

#29-1の涎掛けは、首周りのところに八卦紋が刺繍され、そのほかのところに、仏の手、蝶、如意雲紋などのめでたい文様も施されています。

#29-2は、花びらの形をしていて、八卦の文様のみ刺繍されています。

Fig . #29-2

30

哪吒

＃30是一件套兜在傜族小孩頸上的圍飾，除了精緻的刺繡之外，樹子、古琉璃、流蘇都具有驅邪招福的意義；不過在頸圍中間被兩隻蝴蝶夾著的銅片，像是紅孩兒哪吒，他乘著風火輪，手提著一根武器棒，不僅代表了無限的精力，也有祝福孩子永遠吉祥健康的意義。

紅孩兒哪吒在《封神榜》中是鐵扇公主、牛魔王的兒子，另一傳說則是說他為唐朝李靖和紅拂女所生。

哪吒，源於元代《三教搜神大全》。明代古典小說《西遊記》，《封神演義》中人物。《西遊記》中指哪吒為托塔天王李靖的第三子，形似少年，但神通廣大，曾參與討伐孫悟空，大敗而歸。

《封神演義》說：一日哪吒去東海九灣河沐浴，因將太乙真人所賜寶物「乾坤圈」置水中玩耍，致使東海龍宮動搖不已。龍王急忙差巡海夜叉察看，惹惱哪吒被打死，龍王三太子敖丙再調集龍兵與其大戰，又被哪吒打死，此段情節流傳後世，就是著名的「哪吒大鬧龍宮」。

Na-Ja

This bib is part of the children's wear in the Yao minority tribe. In addition to the refined embroidery in Figure 30, plant seeds, old glass beads and tassels on the bib are all symbols of good fortune. Please notice the image of the legendary Na-Ja between two brass plates in the shape of butterflies. Na-Ja rides on a fiery wheel holding a long golden stick in his hand as his weapon. Na-Ja not only represents an abundance of energy, he also symbolizes good health.

哪吒

傜族の子ともの頸に巻くマフラーの飾り、細かい刺しゅうのほか、木の子、古い琉璃、髪の裾など邪を驅除し、福を招く意味がある．ただし、マフラーの真ん中に二つのチョウチョウに挟まれている一枚の銅は赤いこともの形．それは哪吒という人物であり、かれは風火輪に乗り、手に武器になった棒を持ち、無限の精力を表し、子ともの福と健康を祈る意味である。

Fig．#30

31 如意雲紋

如意原是佛具,在民間則拿來作為搔癢的用具,因此常在古玩的玉器裡見到如意。由於人們嚮往「事事如意」,因此發展成為吉祥物,其頭又與靈芝的形象結合,形成如祥雲凝聚般的如意紋,也稱為「如意雲頭」。

在#31-1的圍兜中,可以清楚看到四個大型的如意雲頭,另外,創作者還繡上花卉、竹、鳥、蜜蜂和蝴蝶,相當美麗。即便在少數民族聚集的壯族部落,如意雲紋也常被人們用來祈求如意吉祥。

#31-2這只壯族的圍兜,便以如意雲紋為主題圖案,並添加花蝶予以襯托,可以看到縫製這只圍兜的壯族婦女,刻意把花與蝴蝶設計成如同如意雲紋般的造型,兩相呼應,如流水行雲般的線條之美,在這裡展露無遺,也顯見婦女的巧思。

Fig·#31-1

As You Wish—*Ru-yi*

Ru-yi is shaped like a long bar and its head looks like a sword guard. In ancient time it was used for self-defense and for back scratching. *Ru-yi* was also an emblem of Buddhism, and its presence functions as a talisman to ward off evils. *Ru-yi* literally means "attaining what one desires." It is often given as a gift, signifying well wishes and prosperity for the recipient.

In Figure 31-1, we can clearly see the four shapes of the *ru-yi* cloud heads, in addition to embroidery of flowers, bamboo, birds, bees, and butterflies, which are all signs of good fortune.

Fig . #31-2

「如意雲」の文様

如意はもともと仏教の道具の一つです。民間の人は形を真似したものを作り、背中の痒い時にはそれで掻いたりして、大変重宝していました。このため、今でも古物商で見かけます。如意は中国語では「事事如意」として、「万事順調に進む」という意味を持っていますので、縁起物の一つになりました。さらに如意の頭の部分は、瑞雲が集まっているように見えるため、「如意雲紋」と呼ばれ、「如意雲頭」とも呼ばれるようになりました。

#31-1には、大きな如意雲頭が4つあり、花、竹、鳥、蜂、蝶などが散らばっていて、大変美しいものであります。中国の少数民族である「壮族」の村でも、この如意雲の文様は、「万事順調に進む」ようにと祈る祈願によく使われます。

#31-2は、壮族のもので、如意の文様を取り入れています。そのほかの花や蝶の飾りも、如意の形に合わせて同じような形をしています。この涎掛けには、美しい文様の、流れるような線が随所に見られ、創意工夫を凝らした傑作です。

(32)

回紋

回紋是由「回」字相連接所形成的幾何圖形，也稱為「回回錦」。在商周時代的青銅器上，人們已開始用此紋作為器皿上的地紋，有連接不斷的意思。

在＃32這件收集自廣西一帶的圍兜上，我們可以在圍兜下方垂墜的口袋邊上，看到綿延不絕的回字紋織帶，用以帶來吉祥的徵候，另外，在圍兜頭項下繡著垂掛著祈求孩兒長命富貴的長命鎖，整體來說，是比較少見的圍兜造型。

The Revolving Pattern

The thunder, or meander, pattern can be found on bronzes from as early as the Shang period (16th – 11th centuries B.C.). Its continuous and repetitive pattern has the connotation of endlessness and is associated with clouds and the rolling of thunder. The revolving pattern in Figure 32, the bib from Guangxi, showcases a thunder pattern all around the edges of the pocket of the bib. Right below the neck of the bibs is a "longevity lock" motif.

回字紋

回字紋は、「回」の字を延々と繋げた幾何学文様で、「回回錦」とも呼ばれます。約3000年前の殷の時代に、この文様はすでに銅器の下地に飾りとして使われていました。「断絶することがない」というめでたい意味をもっているからです。

#32は、広西辺りから収集した作品で、大きな前掛けが袋になっていて、その袋の縁にめでたい回字紋が見られます。涎掛けの胸の部分に錠の文様があります。これは「長生き」を意味しますが、滅多に見かけない珍しいものです。

Fig．#32

銅錢紋

銅錢的鑄造，在中國已有兩千多年的歷史，古銅錢雖然已不是流通的貨幣，但在民間常將此種古幣以紅線串起縫在孩子的衣飾，讓他穿戴，或在衣飾上繡上銅錢的符號，以求「招財」。

而且古銅錢是外圓內方的形制，也有勉勵孩子，對外做人圓融，而對自己要求方正規矩的用意。銅錢常和蝙蝠一起出現，寓意「福（蝠）在眼前（錢）」。

#33-1為河北一帶的圍兜作品，以貼布手法做成，推估年代約在十九世紀，圍兜上繡有多枚外圓內方的銅錢紋，錯落有致，另外加上如意雲紋，取「雲」與「運」諧音，有「福運」的含意。

#33-2是黎平侗族的少數民族作品，在圍兜下方四方形的布片正中央，繡有多枚銅錢紋，在銅錢紋周邊則環繞著四隻蝙蝠，寓意：「蝠（福）在眼錢（前）」。另在頸項邊緣和圍兜四邊均飾有如意雲紋。

The bib in Figure 33-2 is from the Dong minority group in Li-ping. In the center of the bib, there is square filled with coins and around this square are four bats. Because the pronunciation of "bat" (*fu*) in Chinese is the same is that of "fortune," (*fu*) and the pronunciation of "money" (*qian*) is the same as that of "before" (*qian*) or "in front of," this particular combination of symbols means that "fortune is right before one's eyes."

Coins

Chinese coins have a history of more than 2,000 years. As a symbol of prosperity, Chinese coins have always been popular—both as amulets and as ornaments. Because the original coins were round with square holes punched out in the middle, the idea was that children who wore coins as ornaments or had them sewn onto clothing would be able to have a well-rounded personality towards others, but would be able to be strict and rigid with themselves.

The bib in Figure 33-1 is from Hebei and uses the appliqué method. As you can see, the embroidery is of a series of coins—round with square cutouts in the center—all around the perimeter of the bib.

Fig・#33-1

銅銭紋

中国の銅銭鋳造は2000年以上の歴史を持っています。古銭はもう随分前から流通していませんが、民間ではよく赤い糸を通して子供の首に付けたり、子供の服などにその文様を縫いつけたりして、我が子の財運を祈りました。

また古銭は真ん中に四角い穴が開いており、周りは丸い形をしているので、「自分には謹厳、人には寛大」という子供への戒めの意味も込められています。古銭はよく蝙蝠(コウモリ)と対で文様になっており、「幸せは直ぐ眼の前にある」という意味を表しています。

#33-1は、河北辺りの19世紀前後の作品で、アップリケの技法を採っています。古銭と如意雲の文様を組み合わせた、幸運を祈るという意味の涎掛けです。

#33-2は、黎平地方の侗族という少数民族の作品です。大きな四方形の涎掛けの真ん中には、沢山の古銭が刺繍されてあり、その周りを4匹の蝙蝠(コウモリ)が囲んでいます。これは「裕福になりますように」との願いがこめられたものです。首周りと蝙蝠の回りには如意雲の文様が施されています。

Fig . #33-2

㉞

長命鎖

中國人都希冀長命百歲，認為長壽是人生很大的福氣，但怎樣可以長壽呢？中國人相信鎖可以鎖住命神，因此長久下來便發展出長命鎖，藉此來永保孩兒長命百歲，為人父母者認為這正是給初生兒最好的禮物。

民間還流傳一種「百家鎖」，父母從一百位不同的親戚朋友處要來小銅錢，再加上自己的湊足了份量，重新融化打模鑄成長命鎖，將鎖掛在孩兒的頸上鎖住長命。這樣的習俗，展現為人父母對孩兒無止盡的掛念與深切祝福。

＃34-1的圍兜，在四片葉片上分別繡上了四個相當精緻的長命鎖，鎖的造型相當美麗而且繁複，帶有點如意雲紋的味道，可以想見，縫製這只圍兜的媽媽，是多麼細心地注入己身的盼望與祝福。另外，這只圍兜的配色以紅色為底，襯上黑、紫、粉紅和綠色，鎖和鎖之間兩兩成對，顯得既出色又高貴。

＃34-2則化繁為簡，藍紫色的底布上，在頸項處懸掛一個寫有長命字樣的長命鎖。這樣簡單的形式，透露出這只圍兜可能並非出自富裕之家，正因如此，也傳凸顯為人父母者無論貧富，同樣對自己兒女寄予深深祝福的用心。

The Longevity Lock

The Chinese have long considered longevity to be the most sought after of fortunes. But how does one attain longevity? The Chinese believe that the symbol of the lock will help secure one's life and grant him longevity, so the "longevity lock" has long been used as an auspicious charm, often as a gift or as an ornament on clothing.

Another folk charm is the "hundred family lock," which is obtained by the parents going around to friends and family, collecting a few coins from each, then melting down the coins to cast a lock for their children. This lock assures that the child—with the blessing from one hundred close friends and family—will live a long and prosperous life.

On the bib in Figure 34-1, there are four longevity locks that also look like cloud motifs. This doubling of motifs is quite clever, and with its red background and black, magenta, and green colors, it is an eye-catching and unique work of art.

In comparison, the design of the bib in Figure 34-2 is much more simple and straight-forward, using the characters for "longevity lock" to represent the lock itself.

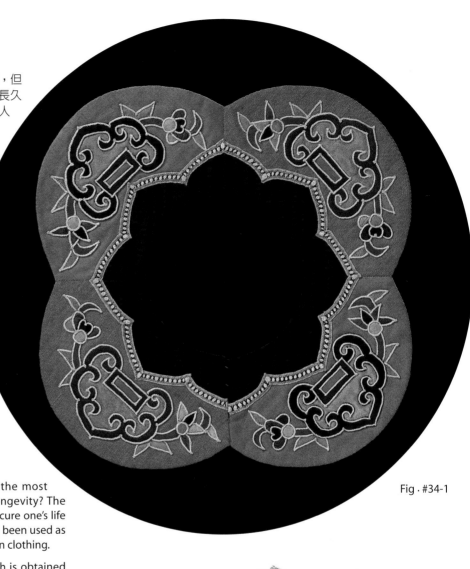

Fig . #34-1

長生きを祈る錠

長生きとは誰もが願うことだと思いますが、中国人ももちろん例外ではありません。中国人は錠によって、命を繋ぎ止めることが出来ると信じていました。そのため、長生きの象徴として「長命錠」が流行するようになりました。生まれたばかりの我が子への何よりの贈り物だと親は思ったのでしょう。

このほか、民間では「百家錠」というものが流行りました。これは、親が百人の親戚から集めてきた小さな銅銭に、自らの分も足し鋳造し直して作った「長命錠」の一種で、子供の首に掛けて長生きを祝福するものです。

#34-1は、四枚の半円形の布地に、四つの精緻な長命錠が刺繍されております。錠の形が綺麗で、相当芸の細かいものと言えます。また錠の形をしていながら、如意雲の形にも似せており、二つの祝福を我が子に寄せる親心が伺えます。

同じ錠の文様でも、#34-2は大変素朴で、質素な家のものだと思われます。貧富の差こそ有れ、子を思う親心は変わらないということが、改めて思い知らされた作品です。

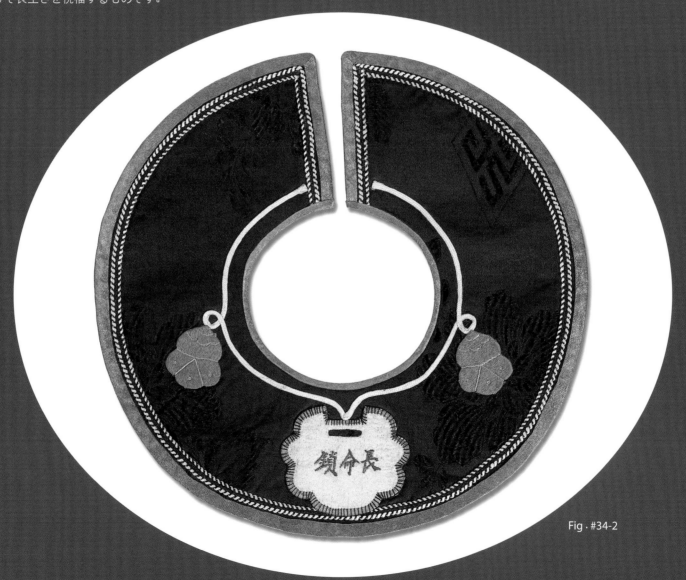

Fig・#34-2

燈籠紋

以各種材料（竹、木、金屬等）製造燈籠的手藝，可能從漢朝便開始了。除了有照明的功能之外，燈籠也是民間有喜慶活動時所用的項目。「張燈結彩」就是形容歡欣鼓舞的景象。在圍兜上繡上燈籠，自然也是代表了興高采烈的情緒了。

＃35是黎平侗族的作品，上頭繁多的紋飾，包含了長命富貴字樣、萬字紋、壽字紋、走龍和燈籠紋，以垂直長串的方式組成整組的圖樣，充滿喜氣洋洋的節慶氣氛。圖案全以白色繡線繡成，在黑色底布的反襯下，凸顯了明朗簡約的風格。

灯篭紋

竹、木、金属類など、様々の材料で灯篭を作る手工芸は、漢の時代から始まったそうです。照明としての役割のほか、灯篭は昔から民間の行事で活躍をしていました。中国の人々は、おめでたい事がある度に、よく赤々と灯る灯篭を軒下に下げたり、赤い布で作った花を玄関などに飾ったりして、雰囲気を出していました。この涎掛けに刺繍された灯篭が、喜びの象徴であることはいうまでもないでしょう。

#35は黎平侗族の作品で、長生きを意味する「長命富貴」の言葉、「萬」の字や「寿」の字、龍、灯篭などの文様が賑やかに飾られ、めでたい雰囲気をたっぷりと出しています。文様のラインは全て白い糸で刺繍され、黒い生地との対比により、シンプルで明るい感じを与えています。

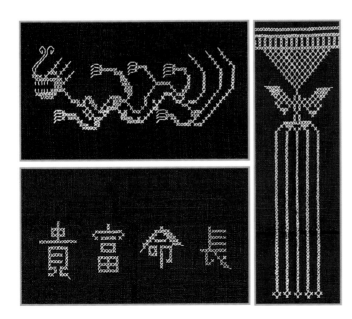

Lanterns

The making of lanterns from such materials as bamboo, wood, and gold probably started in the Han period. Aside from its practical purpose of lighting, the lantern was often used during extremely happy events—such as the birth of a child. In Figure 35, the bib is from the Dong tribe in Li-ping and it boasts many fortunate motifs—there is the symbol for longevity and a walking dragon, both of which are part of a hanging lantern, announcing the happy event (in this case, the arrival of a baby.)

Fig . #35

36

人紋

看到人和人一個接一個地手拉手，讓人不禁聯想到節慶時的載歌載舞。人紋、燈籠紋、花盆、鳥、魚，都代表喜慶之意，可歸類為慶典紋飾。其實人紋可以追溯到原始彩陶上的紋樣，看到一個人接一個人地做舞蹈的姿勢。少數民族的圖案中，也特別喜歡採用人紋。傳說人紋有生殖、招魂與避邪的寓意，也有喜慶、團結、歡樂的象徵。

這件圍兜，在藍色的底布上有非常精彩的人形圖案，值得細細欣賞。細看＃36的圍兜，若分成上下兩段來看，可以明顯看到上半部以燈籠紋飾為主，下方則散佈了非常多的人形紋，除了一個個張手排列，做出舞蹈歡呼的模樣，每一個人的頭上也都梳著造型奇特的髮型，身著紅色衣裙。吉慶的燈籠紋，加上舉手歡呼的人形紋，更增添歡樂氣氛。

另外，這只圍兜面上還散佈了各式各樣的鳥、魚、蝴蝶、星星圖飾，看來既美麗又豐富。

Human Figures

The image of seeing people joining hands will inevitably make one think of people dancing and singing during times of celebration. This image, as a motif, can be traced back to paintings on Neolithic ceramics. In minority tribal art, the use of this image is also very prevalent as it has the connotation of reproduction, celebration, and happiness.

There is a lot of activity on the bib in Figure 36. When examined closely, we see that the bib can be separated into two distinct parts—the first is the large motif of the hanging lantern, and the second is the embroidery of many little people joining hands in song and dance. Not only are the people standing with outstretched arms in jubilation, they are all having special hair style and red costumes, which adds to the celebratory nature of the bib. In addition, there are embroideries of all sorts of creatures, such as birds, fish, butterflies, and stars, which give this bib a feeling of abundance and joy.

Fig . #36

人間紋

大勢の人が手を繋いでいて、さらに灯篭、鳥、魚などのめでたい文様が有ることを見ると、これは明らかに楽しいお祭りの場面なのでしょう。人間の文様は、原始時代の土器――「彩陶」に遡ることが出来ます。それには、人々が手を繋ぎ、楽しそうに踊っている姿が描かれていました。また少数民族は人間の文様を好んで使う傾向があります。人間紋には、子孫繁栄、厄払い、魂を呼ぶなどの意味が込められ、またお祝い、喜び、団欒の象徴でもあります

この作品は、地味な紺の生地に、精細な文様が散らばり、見応えのある一点です。絵は上、下の二段に分かれており、上の段は灯篭紋が主で、下の段は、多くの人々が両手を挙げ、踊っている姿が見られます。また全員頭にユニークなヘアスタイルで、赤い服を身につけていて、楽しいお祭りの雰囲気が伝わってきます。更に様々な鳥、魚、蝶、星の飾りも賑やかで美しいものです。

37

吉祥字

中國文字本身的造型，本就是「美的安排」，書法藝術是其一，若母親把帶有祝福意義的文字繡在圍兜上，更是直接表達了為孩兒求福添壽，祈求功名富貴的心情。在中國，除了吉祥神、吉祥物外，在生活中也多見吉祥字，單單吉祥字數就推測約有兩百多個。在這裡可以看到的多見於小朋友的衣件裡，如：長命富貴＃37-1、壽字＃37-2等等。

＃37-3的圍兜作品，以十字繡來表現，上頭繡著「福壽康寧」四個吉祥字，而在圍兜下方則繡有鳴啼的公雞，象徵「功名富貴」。

＃37-4在八個圍兜的葉片上，分別繡有「海屋添籌，春秋不老」八個吉祥字，有關「海屋添籌」的由來，相傳在渤海東的大島上有聖山華屋，有一次有三位老人互相問年紀，其中一位說：「若海水變桑田時，我就添歲。」所以，「海屋添籌」即有「多壽」的意思。

Fig . #37-1

Fig . #37-2

Auspicious Characters: **Longevity, Health, Peace, and Fortune**

Chinese characters are about the "beauty of arrangement," and the ultimate form of this discipline is the art of Chinese calligraphy. When calligraphic characters are stitched onto clothing, it is a very direct translation of the mother's hopes and dreams for her child. In addition to auspicious symbols and motifs, Chinese characters that have fortunate meanings are also regarded with much respect. In Figure 37-1 and Figure 37-2, the characters for longevity are stitched onto the bibs. It is easy to infer what these mothers wanted most for their children.

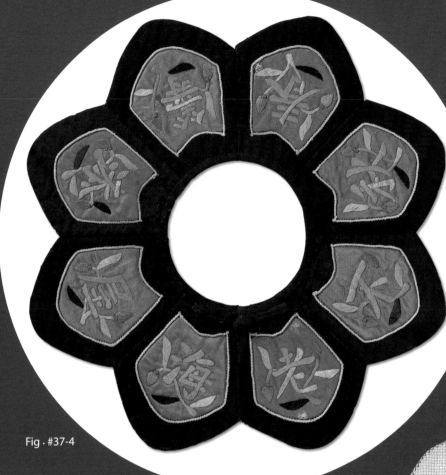

Fig . #37-4

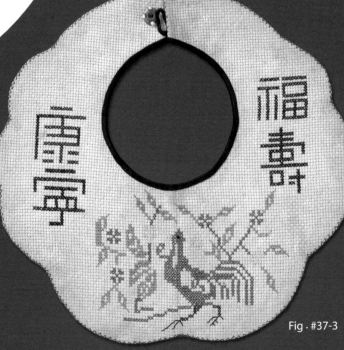

Fig . #37-3

めでたい四字熟語

中国では縁起のいい神、縁起のいい物のほかに、日常生活でも縁起のいい言葉が豊富にあります。また書道からでも判るように、中国の文字はそれ自体美しい芸術だと言えましょう。そのため、我が子の健康と出世を願う母親は、よく祝福の意味を込めた文字を、我が子の涎掛けに飾りました。

縁起のいい言葉は推定だけで二百以上にも上ります。#37-1の「長命富貴」、

#37-2の「寿」などは、よく子供の着るものに施される言葉です。

#37-3は、クロスステッチの技法を駆使したものです。「福寿康寧」という祝福の言葉の下に、啼いている雄鶏があり、これには「出世」という意味が込められています。

#37-4は、八枚からなる生地の上に、「海屋添籌、春秋不老」という「長生き」を意味するめでたい言葉が並んでいます。

Using the cross-stitching technique, the bib in Figure 37-3 has the characters for "fortune," "longevity," "health," and "peace" stitched on it. Below them is the rendering of a crowing rooster, wishing children to be as diligent and as faithful as a rooster who wakes up a village every morning.

In Figure 37-4, on the eight petals of the bib, there are eight different characters that, together, form a saying that wishes the wearer a long life.

第壹部 幼兒的第一件衣裳─圍兜

38

抽象的圖案

抽象的圖案，特別在少數民族的圍兜上可見。也許是花草、蔓卷、樹藤等大自然的形象予以抽象化。

#38-1收集自安徽一帶，似乎像捲曲的藤蔓。#38-2在用色和圖案上顯得大膽奔放，令人印象深刻，另外採用貼布技法，也值得欣賞。

#38-3的圍兜，以極細的十字繡，展現出抽象的幾何圖形，可以想見當初縫製這只圍兜的婦女，是多麼地專注和富有耐心，令人動容。

Abstract Motifs

Abstract images are especially common in works from minority people. The designs of Figure 38-1 may be derived from flowers, grass, trees, and other objects of nature. The design of Figure 38-2 is bold, as is the use of colors. It leaves a lasting impression. The detail of Figure 38-3 is achieved by using careful cross-stitching. The care and concentration put into this bib are deeply moving.

Fig·#38-1

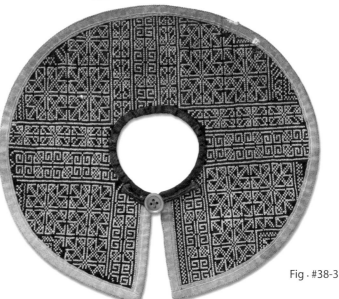

Fig·#38-3

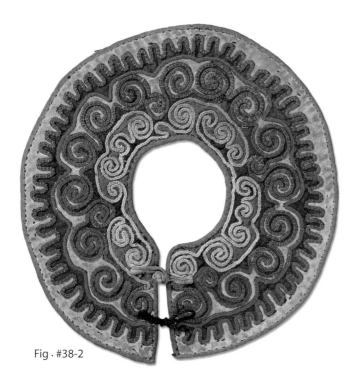

Fig·#38-2

抽象の図案

花、草、蔓などを抽象化した文様は、特に少数民族の涎掛けによく見かけます。#38-1は、安徽辺りから収集したもので、図案は曲がった藤のように見えます。#38-2の色使いや文様には、大胆で奔放な雰囲気が感じられます。またアップリケの技法も見どころです。

#38-3はとても細かいクロスステッチで、抽象的で幾何学的な図形を表しています。この涎掛けを手がけた女性が、辛抱強く刺繍に取り組む姿が眼に浮かび、感心せずにはいられないものです。

Part I ① Wei Zwei—The Bib　最初章— 幼児の第一枚目の衣装—涎掛け

第②部 兜兜情事—肚兜

Part II --- *Du Dou* – The Undergarment

第二部--- 恋物語にまつわる腹掛けの文様

絲竹之美 Chapter 1 Stories from Chinese Opera
第一章 恋物語

㊴

《拾玉鐲》

中國戲曲精緻豐美，在民間也是廣為流傳，是舊時人們很重要的精神食糧與日常娛樂來源，細心地婦女們將這些引人入勝的戲曲故事繡在孩兒的衣著上，既寬慰了自己，也為小寶寶的未來，添加了幾許人生舞台的豐富顏色。

＃39這件肚兜收集自山西一帶，酒紅絲緞上，上方繡的是戲曲《法門寺》之第一折《拾玉鐲》，下方則是《殺狗勸妻》的民間故事，採用的均是細緻的貼布繡。

明代時，眉鄔地區少女孫玉姣與母親相依為命，以養雞維持生活。有一天，母親前往普陀庵聽經，玉姣把雞群放出，獨自到門口做針線活。青年傅朋閒遊，路過孫家門口，見玉姣美貌生愛慕之心，便借買雞之名上前答話。因母親不在，玉姣做不了主，買賣做不成，傅朋只好說再往別家買雞。

傅朋見玉姣已經進院，自己仍不捨離去。這時玉姣開門探視，兩人對望，羞得玉姣急忙掩門。傅朋知玉姣對自己有意，便把母親贈給他的一對玉鐲取出一只，見左右無人把它放在門前，然後敲敲門環躲在一邊。

玉姣聞聲開門，見地上有只玉鐲，想是剛才見到的那位後生送她的，猶豫再三，終於把它撿起。這時傅朋忽然出現在面前，羞得她急忙還鐲，而傅朋把玉鐲留給了她。這一切被鄰居劉婆所見，她故意與玉姣打趣，追問玉鐲的來歷，玉姣羞而不答。劉婆徵得玉姣的同意，決定為她和傅朋之間牽線搭橋。

傳統京劇有《雙玉鐲》整本戲，也常以折子戲方式演出，是很受歡迎的戲碼。下方的《殺狗勸妻》是因妻虐婆婆，丈夫殺狗戒之。這名刺繡的婦女將戲曲中的人物表現的靈巧而生動。

Picking Up a Jade Bracelet and Kill the Dog to Warn the Wife

The stories of Chinese opera and folk tales have passed on from generation to generation because they bring color and theatricality to people's lives. Women will often embroider scenes or characters from these stories as a way to continue passing on these stories to their children, as well as add color to their children's lives.

The undergarment in Figure 39 is from Shanxi. The two characters embroidered on the top half of the undergarment are from the opera *Picking up a Jade Bracelet* and the characters on the bottom half are from the folk tale *Kill the Dog to Warn the Wife*.

Picking up a Jade Bracelet is about a girl named Yu Jiao, who lives with her mother and takes care of a chicken coop for a living. One day, Yu Jiao has an encounter with a young man, who is immediately taken with her. He makes an excuse to look at the chickens so that he can see Yu Jiao again. Back then, young girls weren't allowed to be alone with boys, so Yu Jiao tells him that her mother is not home and she closes the door. To show his admiration for Yu Jiao, the boy leaves a set of jade bracelets on her doorstep, knocks on the door, and quickly runs away. As soon as Yu Jiao picks up the bracelet, the boy shows up. She is embarrassed, but the boy convinces her to accept the bracelet as a token of their engagement. Nearby, an old grandmother witnesses the whole scene and eventually becomes their matchmaker. This opera describes the delicate push and pull between a man and a woman.

Kill the Dog to Warn the Wife is about a man who goes away for business and while he's away, his wife mistreats his mother. When he returns, he kills the dog as a warning to his wife.

Fig . #39

微笑ましい男女の出会い―拾玉鐲

中国の演劇は、演目も多く演出が多彩で、たくさんの人々を魅了してきました。恐らく母親たちもそれに惹かれ、面白い話を我が子の着るものに再現してみたのでしょう。#39の涎掛けは、山西から収集したもので、ワインレッドの生地に二つの場面が描かれています。上の図柄は、微笑ましい男女の出会いを描く「拾玉鐲」という話で、下の図柄は、姑を苛める嫁を改心させる「殺狗勧妻」という話からです。いずれもアツプリケによるもので、大変生き生きとしています。

④ 《天仙配》

《天仙配》是一個膾炙人口的民間故事。話說，東漢人董永家窮喪父，賣身以求葬父，曾遇一女子，兩人戀愛結婚，並協同到債主家當奴僕，錢主要求董永的太太織布三百匹以償債，而董妻居然在一個月內就飛快地織完，使董永得以贖身。這下董妻才告訴董永，她原來是天上的織女，因奉天命，來幫助孝子董永，話說完，就凌空而去，這就是民間戲劇中著名的《天仙配》。後來，董妻在天上生了一子，送還給董永，傳說中這位天仙配所生的兒子，就是大儒董仲舒。

＃40這只收集自中國北方的肚兜，以正紅的絲緞為底，顯得喜氣洋洋。肚兜正中央繡有《天仙配》故事，可以看到一名官人與一名女子在畫面左右，女子手中抱了一個嬰孩，官人在右接應，兩人中間隔了一座橋和一隻大蝴蝶，天上有雲，兩旁有竹子，橋下有象徵性的水流及魚，細緻的刺繡，將這個天上人間的浪漫故事，表現的份外引人入勝。

Encounter with a Fairy

Dong Yong is so poor that he doesn't have money to bury his own father. So he sells himself as a slave in order to appropriately pay respect to his father. Moved by Dong Yong's filial piety, a weaving fairy becomes a human in order to marry him to help him undo his contract of servitude. The fairy tells Dong Yong's master that she can weave, so the master makes an impossible request, which the fairy fulfills overnight. Dong Yong is freed and the fairy's time on earth is up, so she returns to heaven. While in heaven, she gives birth to a boy and sends the boy down to Dong Yong. The boy eventually becomes a famous Han Dynasty scholar.

In the embroidery of Figure 40, we see the fairy on the top left, holding her baby. Heaven and earth are separated by a bridge, and Dong Yong stands at the bottom of the bridge.

中国版の竹取物語—天仙配

＃40の「天仙配」の話は、まさに中国版の竹取物語です。二人の主人公が向き合い、女性の手には赤ん坊が抱かれています。このロマンチックな場面は、真っ赤な色の生地に、蝶、雲、竹、河、魚が飾られ、一層喜ばしい雰囲気が出ています。精緻な刺繍も見逃せないものです。

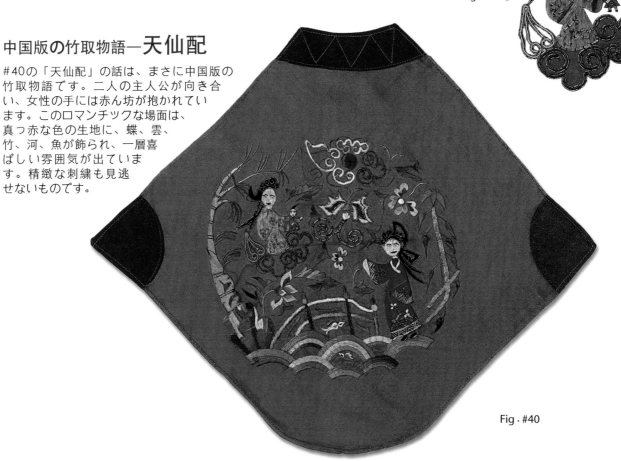

Fig.＃40

《桑園會》

《桑園會》又名《秋胡戲妻》。戰國時，魯人秋胡在楚國為光祿大夫，回家省親。其妻羅敷，在丈夫離家後的二十年中，和婆婆以養蠶度日。一天，羅敷到桑園採桑，恰巧預見回鄉的秋胡。秋胡雖然見到採桑女像是自己的妻子，卻不敢貿然相認，於是下馬故意向她打聽秋胡的住處，並假稱自己與秋胡有八拜之交，因給胡秋送信來到此地。羅敷見有了丈夫的下落並有萬金家書送到，非常高興，但不講明自己就是胡秋之妻，只聲稱是秋胡的鄰居。

羅敷聽來人把自己家中事講得明明白白，才告知自己就是秋胡之妻。秋胡大喜，但想自己離家日久，不明妻子是否貞節，於是假稱秋胡在楚國已另娶，並對她加以調戲，以馬蹄金一錠試探妻子之心。羅敷怒斥秋胡而逃去。

秋胡回到家中，母親見到久別的兒子，又得知他在楚國做了高官，歡喜異常。羅敷被婆婆喚出，見調戲自己的竟是丈夫，憤然自縊，秋胡母子急忙相救。母親知道真相後痛責秋胡，秋胡悔恨不已，屈膝請罪，夫妻終於言歸於好。

＃41這只肚兜，在口袋上繡以《桑園會》故事，可以看到畫面中一名女子在桑樹旁，肩上挑著採好的桑葉，身旁不遠處立著一名官人，巧妙地點出《桑園會》的故事情節。

Rendezvous at Mulberry Garden

In Figure 41, the image on the bib tells a story from the Spring/Autumn period (a 2,500 year-old story). A man leaves home to study in order to serve in the high court. His wife and mother grow a big mulberry garden to nurture silkworms so as to earn a living. Twenty years later, the man gets the position in high court and finally returns home. But it's been so long that his wife doesn't recognize him. The husband tests his wife and teases her. She gets angry and tells him that she already has a husband and asks him to leave her alone. The husband continues to test her—he offers her money and tells her that her husband has already remarried. But she refuses the money.

The husband is happy that his wife has remained loyal after twenty years, and finally reveals himself to his mother. The wife overhears and becomes angry that he doubted her loyalty. She threatens to kill herself, but the mother convinces her to forgive her husband and they have a happy family reunion in the end.

20年ぶりの夫婦再会—桑園会

「桑の園での再会」は、節婦にまつわる昔話です。#41の涎掛けは、桑の木の下で、採れた桑の葉を肩に担いでいる妻と、20年ぶりに帰ってきた夫が描かれています。この物語に聞き覚えのある人は、絵を見た瞬間、「桑の園での再会」だと、すぐピンとくるでしょう。

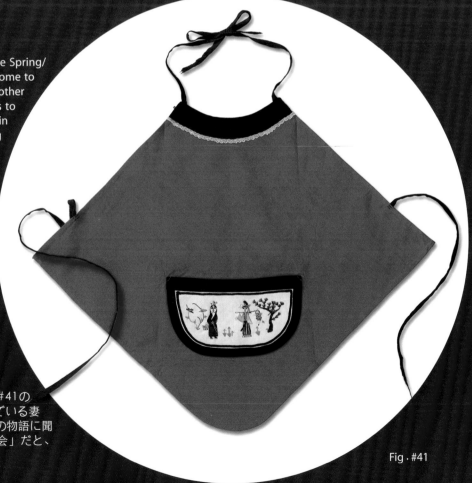

Fig . #41

㊷ 《麥仁罐》

這只肚兜為山西一帶的作品,作品正中央繡的是戲曲《麥仁罐》中的故事人物。

《麥子罐》為民間戲曲《十四王帶箭》其中之折子戲,描述東漢末興時,劉秀遭王莽追殺隻身逃亡,途中飢渴,遇送飯村姑以麥粒粥給他吃,造成情緣。後來劉秀登基後為漢光武帝,即娶村姑為皇后。

♯42肚兜好像就在描述這個故事,上面可以看見一人站立,身旁蹲著的村姑正彎腰從地上的食物籃中舀取麥粒粥,並伸手遞給另外一人,兩人身後繡有美麗的花朵。

Oatmeal Canister

In Figure 42, a would-be king was defeated during combat so he flees to the countryside. A village girl made hot oatmeal to help him. His army eventually wins the battle so he becomes a Han Dynasty king, but even as king, he doesn't forget this country girl's generosity towards him, so he marries her.

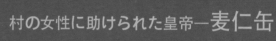

村の女性に助けられた皇帝—麦仁缶

山西からの作品で、真ん中にいるのは「麦仁缶」という昔話に登場する男女です。これは2000年前の、漢の時代の武帝という皇帝が国を起こす前のお話で、敵に追われ逃亡中だったとき、見知らぬ村の女性が、麦粥を食べさせてくれました。のちに皇帝になった彼は、その女性の恩に報いるため、皇后にしたという心暖まる話です。#42には、麦粥の用意を整え、武帝のもとに運ぼうとする二人の村の女性の姿があります。

Fig . #42

第章

民間故事與神話 Chapter 2 Folktales and Fairytales
第二章　民間昔話と神話

(43)

劉海戲蟾

看看＃43的肚兜，一名男子手上拿著一根綁著銅錢的絲線，絲線下有隻抬頭仰望的蟾蜍，引人好奇這是什麼故事？原來蟾蜍在中國人心中是很有靈氣的，傳說中，月亮裡就有一隻蟾蜍，所以中國人叫月亮為「玉蟾」，而銅錢釣蟾蜍則和一則神話故事有關。

相傳，這隻三隻腳的金蟾，是神仙劉海的寵物，有一天，蟾蜍跑掉了，跳到一口古井裡，怎麼喚也喚不回來，劉海靈機一動，想起這隻蟾蜍平日最喜歡咬錢，於是就用絲線綁上銅錢，果然就輕易地把這隻三隻腳的金蟾給釣起來了。從此以後，人們不只認為蟾蜍有靈氣，甚至相信三隻腳的蟾蜍可以帶來財運。

＃43的肚兜繡上劉海戲蟾的民間故事，應該也和求財運有關，我們可以看見劉海釣蟾蜍的動作表現得相當生動，劉海腳下還有幾朵雲，顯示他的仙人身份，蟾蜍下方則是漾漾的水波，表示蟾蜍身在古井中。

Liu Hai Fishes for the Three-legged Toad

Liu Hai has the power to fish with a line upon which hang coins to capture a three-legged frog, which people believe will bring big fortune. (Figure 43)

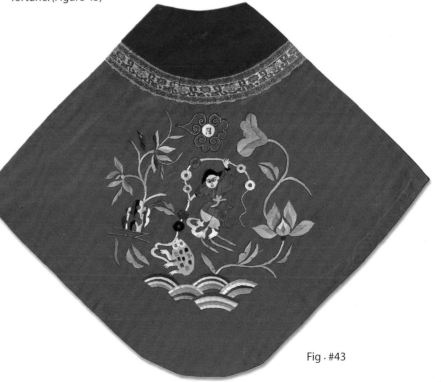

劉海仙人と蟾蜍の話

#43の腹掛けには、古銭を糸で通して手に持っている男性がいて、足元には三本足の蟾蜍(ヒキガエル)が彼を見上げています。この場面は、古い井戸に逃げた蟾蜍を、劉海という仙人が古銭で釣ったという昔話によるものです。それ以来特に三本足の蟾蜍は、「財運をもたらす」縁起物として人気が有ります。蟾蜍の下に波紋があるのは、井戸の中をイメージしています。

Fig . #43

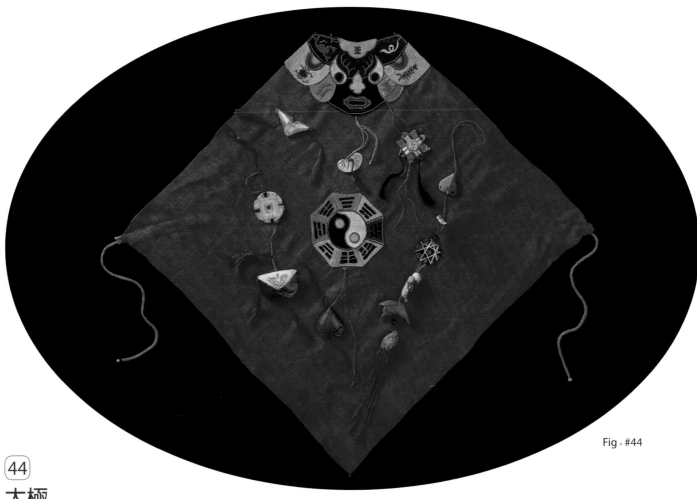

Fig. #44

(44)

太極

#44的肚兜上，裝飾有許多驅毒避邪的吉祥物，首先映入眼簾的是肚兜正中央的太極圖案，太極是一種自渾沌無極之中脫出的陰陽和諧狀態，由太極可以分出陰、陽兩種相對現象，他們是宇宙間所有互為表裡的關係。所謂：「太極生兩儀，兩儀生四象，四象生八卦」，因此又有八卦圖案環繞在太極之四周；而中國人同時認為太極是萬物萌生的開始，因此這個八卦環繞太極的圖案也帶有生生不息的吉祥意涵。

Tai-Chi

The drawing of the Tai-Chi in Figure 44 was commonly surrounded by the Eight Trigrams. Tai-Chi represents a balance of the two genders. Harmony and balance (equality) are the two foundations of human relations. Tai-Chi also has the power of chasing away and warding off evils.

在肚兜上垂掛有一串串小飾物，從香包、蟬、小人偶、果仁、銅錢到菱角，包羅萬象型態各異，相當豐富而可愛。在肚兜頸項處飾有虎頭，虎頭上繡有五毒如蠍子等昆蟲，以為驅毒避邪之用。

宇宙万物の元始を表す—太極

#44には、魔よけや厄払いの意味があるめでたい文様が多く施されています。最も目立っているのは、真ん中にある太極の図案で天地がまだ混沌とし、分かれる以前の宇宙万物の元始を表し、また陰と陽という二つの相対する性質と、宇宙万物の裏表の関係を表す図でもあるとされています。そのため、八卦が太極を囲んでいる文様は、「代々伝承し滅びることがない」といううめでたい意味を持っています。涎掛けの下に、香り袋、蟬、人形、クルミ、コインなど様々な小さな飾りがぶら下がっています。首周りには虎の頭が飾られており、蠍など「五毒」と呼ばれる昆虫が魔よけや厄払いのために刺繍されています。

(45) 麻姑獻壽

麻姑是相傳中的仙女，相傳東漢時曾降臨蔡經家，她「頂中作髻，餘髮垂之及肩」，看來只有十八、九歲，卻極為長壽，因她已目睹東海兩次變為桑田；聽說她能擲米成珠，而且手指像爪，蔡經見過她的手之後，還暗想：「若是抓背癢一定很舒服」。相傳三月三日西王母生日時，麻姑以靈芝釀酒為王母祝壽。

＃45是收集自山西一帶的肚兜作品，在頸項附近有回字紋，肚兜中央則繡有麻姑獻壽的故事，布面上可以看見麻姑前方有一隻梅花鹿，頭頂上則有美麗的蝴蝶翩翩飛舞，腳下花開處處，不知是否正要前往西王母處祝壽。

Ma Gu Presents Gift for Longevity

Ma Gu is a legendary fairy who is famed for longevity. She has lived so long that she has witnessed water becoming land twice. For the birthday of the Mother of the Western Mountain, she used a kind of fungus (ling zhi) to make alcohol. (Figure 45)

西王母の誕生祝い―麻姑献寿

＃45は山西辺りから収集した作品です。首周りの近くに「回字紋」があり、真ん中に「麻姑献寿」、つまり「天女が西王母(最も地位の高い女神)の誕生祝いをする」という神話にまつわる場面が描かれています。天女の前方には鹿がいて、足元には蝶が舞い、花が至る所で咲いています。天女が誕生祝いに出かけていく途中の場面だと思われます。

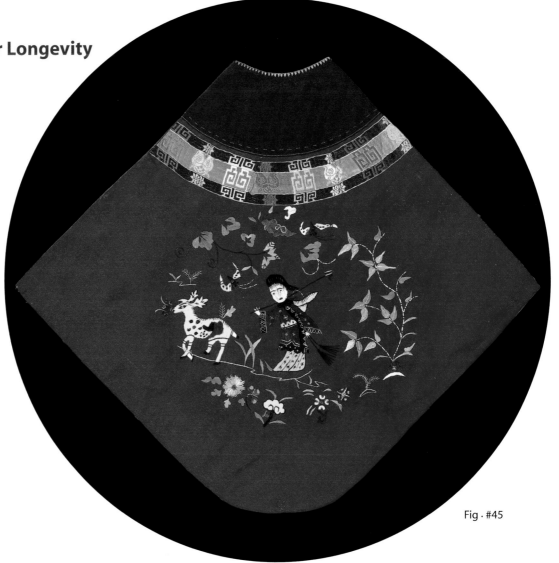

Fig . #45

第 參 章

文人雅風 Chapter 3　Literary Symbolism

第三章　文人の嗜み

(46)

琴棋書畫

中國是禮義之邦，向來崇尚讀書人的文采風流，在為小孩子縫製的貼身衣物中，也不時流露這樣的思緒。＃46是一件相當雅致的肚兜，藍色的底布顯得相當樸素，在頸項處以十字繡繡上了琴棋書畫的圖樣，這些全是古時候文人雅士的書房中必備之物，因此有崇尚雅趣的寓意。

頸項上另繡有「存之肚外」四個字，應當指文人的豁達心境，也以此來期勉孩子胸懷廣闊，無入而不自得。

文人の風雅な嗜み―琴、棋、書、畫

中国人は礼儀を重んじる民族で、特に文人の風雅と文才を高く評価します。子供が使う物にも、時々このような精神が反映されています。＃46は大変雅やかな感じがする一点で、琴、棋、書、画など文人が必ず書斎に置くものをクロスステッチで飾りました。なお、首まわりのところに、「心を広く持つように」という励ましの言葉が書かれています。

Scholarly Pastimes

The Chinese have always held the literary arts in the highest regard. This sentiment is often seen in the embroidery of children's apparel. Figure 46 shows an exceptionally elegant and understated piece. At first glance, the largely indigo undergarment appears to be very simple. Around the collar of the undergarment, there is a rendering of a scroll and a zither – two of the four items that were thought to be indispensable in a scholar's study (the other two are books and chess). It is clear that this mother wanted her child to grow up to have talents in the literary arts.

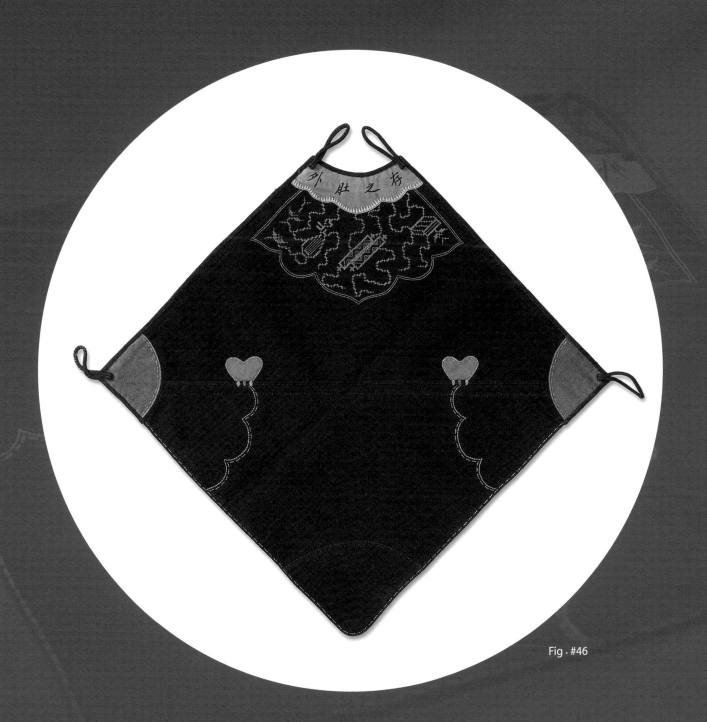

Fig . #46

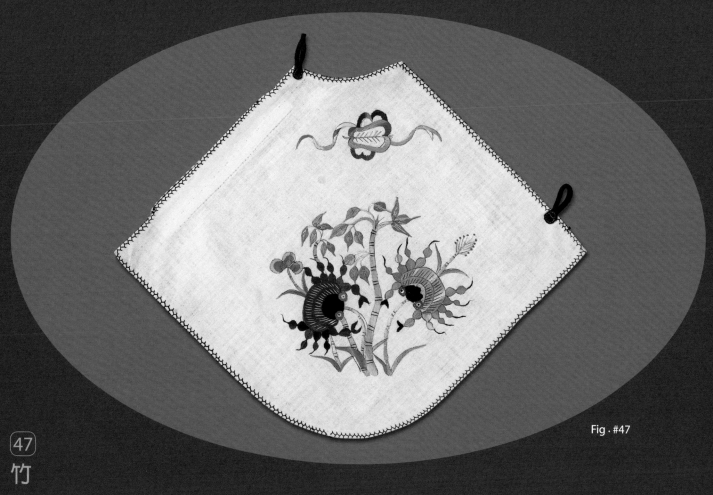

Fig．#47

⑷7

竹

竹子四季常茂，有蓬勃向上的氣質；竹子有節，寓意人品有守；竹子中空，代表謙虛為懷，向來是文人所頌揚的植物。因此，文人有句話說，「寧可食無肉，不可居無竹」，代表了中國文人對竹的喜愛與偏好。

在＃47這件收集自甘肅的肚兜上，可以看到茂盛的竹子挺立正中央，兩旁散佈兩隻螃蟹，下方則有一片芭蕉葉製成的芭蕉扇。蟹為有甲的動物，「甲」是古時科舉的名稱，寓意科舉高中，仕途光明。從肚兜上茂盛的竹子和鮮活的螃蟹來看，母親對孩兒「學而優則仕」的期望不言可喻。

The Bamboo: **A Scholar's Virtues**

The Chinese admire the bamboo for its many symbolic attributes: the bamboo grows in all seasons and is thought to be resilient and strong; it grows straight up into the sky, which represents righteousness; the bamboo is hollow on the inside, which represents modesty and humility because there is space for others; and the bamboo has notches, which symbolizes principles. For these reasons, the bamboo is the scholar's plant. There is a saying that the scholar would rather go without food than without the bamboo.

The undergarment in Figure 47 features beautiful bamboo stalks and two crabs. Because the crab is a symbol of education and the bamboo is a scholarly plant, this mother is hoping that her child will have a bright future in school.

繁盛、節操、出世の象徴—竹

竹は一年中採れるので、「常に繁盛する」という意味が込められています。また節があるので、節操の象徴でもあり、さらに中空なので、謙虚を表し、よく文人に謳歌される植物です。また中国の文人は、「食膳に肉が無くても、住居に竹を欠かすことはできない」というほど、竹に強く心惹かれていました。#47は、甘粛という土地から収集した作品で、繁々とした竹が真ん中に据えられ、両側に生き生きとした蟹が一匹ずついます。この組み合わせは、「文人の出世」を意味するものです。

第肆章

愛的喜悅 Chapter 4 The Joy of Love
第四章 愛の喜び

(48)

鴛鴦戲水

有些肚兜儘管題材為鴛鴦戲水的男女之愛，以尺寸來看仍是屬於小女孩使用的肚兜，而有些描述男女愛情的主題，有時也會出現在小孩的衣飾上。

#48這只肚兜，收集自山東一帶，肚兜正中央，見到一對鴛鴦正在水中嬉戲，旁有花朵，下方是粼粼的水波和蔓生的水草，上方還有飛舞的蝴蝶。鴛鴦一前一後的游著，游在前方的還頻頻回頭，引著心愛的伴侶一同向前，既恩愛又讓人羨慕。整件圍兜以桃紅色為底色，將愛情的喜悅表現的淋漓盡致。

幸せそうに寄り添う鴛鴦—鴛鴦戲水

恋愛を主題とするものは、大人用に使われると限らず、子供物にも見られます。この腹掛けは、山東から収集した作品です。ロマンチックな濃いピンク生地の中央に、一対の鴛鴦が水の中で仲良く戯れています。花、水草、波、蝶に囲まれる中央の鴛鴦は、互いを見つめ合いとても幸せそうです。

Mandarin Ducks Playing in the Water

The subject of love is often embroidered onto children's wear. In Figure 48, there are two mandarin ducks (symbol of a loving couple) swimming in a pond, surrounded by flowers and butterflies. The use of pinks makes this piece especially passionate.

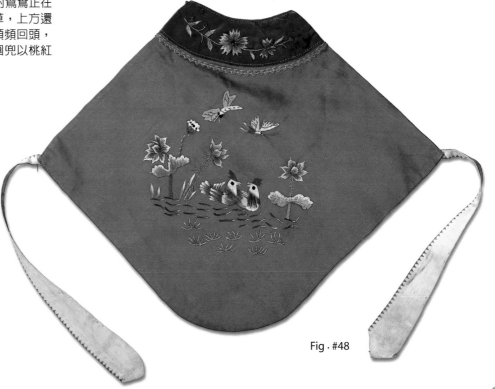

Fig · #48

㊾ 鳳戲牡丹

鳳戲牡丹表現的是對愛情的追求，此題材常在少女思春、幻想愛情的情境中被創造出來。

#49是一件精細華麗的肚兜，繡工的表現相當精彩，整件肚兜佈滿了美麗的紋飾。在肚兜下方是鳳戲牡丹的主題，可以看見兩隻鳳一左一右地隱身在牡丹花叢裡，而作者把牡丹的藤蔓無限延伸，成為攀藤環繞的美麗圖形，牡丹叢中還有翩翩飛舞的蝴蝶，也是象徵美麗愛情的「蝶戀花」。另在肚兜上方可以見到象徵吉祥長壽的壽桃和佛手。

The Phoenix and the Peony

The image of a phoenix and a peony relays the feeling of pursuing love, which is often on the minds of young girls. The spectacular needlework in Figure 49 shows off this theme. There is a pair of phoenixes looking like they are playing a game of hide and go seek in the tendrils of leaves from the beautiful peony. Upon careful examination, we see that there are also dancing butterflies, which too signify love.

男女の愛情の象徴—鳳凰と牡丹

この組み合わせは「男女の愛情」を表しています。男女の愛情に憧れを持つ思春期の少女を描くときに、よく使われる文様です。#49は華麗な腹掛けで、精細な刺繍で描かれた美しい文様にびっしりと埋め尽くされています。下の方は、二匹の鳳凰が牡丹の花の中に見え隠れしていて、牡丹の蔓が優雅な曲線を描いて延びていきます。その間に蝶が飛んでおり、上の方には縁起物の桃と仏の手も見られます。蝶はよく花と対になり「花に恋をする蝶」として、やはり「男女の愛情」を象徴しています。

Fig．#49

多子多孫

石榴被視為吉祥的象徵即因其多籽。在較傳統的社會裡，民間的婚嫁中仍可見到將石榴剝開，露出漂亮的粒粒果籽放在新房裡，以祝新婚夫婦早生貴子，俗稱「榴開百子」。

＃50這件圍兜，可以見到一名童子站立在石榴樹下嬉戲，代表早生貴子，代代相傳的祝福。而在石榴樹上方繡有一隻蝙蝠，有「招福」、「福在眼前」之意，襯在鮮紅的底布上顯得格外喜氣。這件肚兜為甘肅一帶的作品。

Pomegranates: **Many Children and Grandchildren**

Pomegranates also symbolize children. In more traditional Chinese cultures, it is customary to leave a cut-open pomegranate in the newlyweds' room. The gorgeous, bright red, busting seeds teem with life and energy. (Figure 50)

子沢山の石榴—**子孫繁栄**

石榴は種が沢山あることで、縁起物の一つとなりました。今でも古風な家ではお嫁さんを迎える日に、石榴を半分に割り中の真っ赤な種を出し、新郎新婦の部屋に置き、「早く元気な赤ん坊が生まれますように」と祈願する習慣が残っています。甘粛から収集した#50の腹掛けは、石榴の木の下に男の子が立っていて、これは「早く子供が生まれますように」という意味が込められています。また石榴の上に蝙蝠（コウモリ）がいて、これは「幸せが早く来ますように」ということを祈願するもので、赤い生地と共に大変めでたい雰囲気を伝えています。

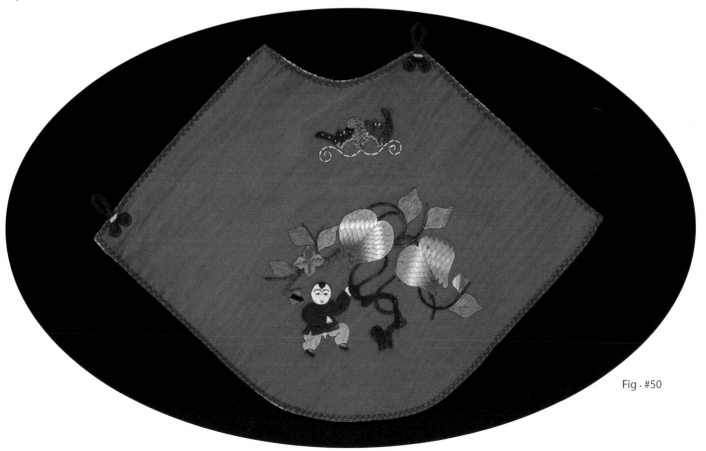

Fig . #50

⑤ 麒麟送子

麒麟是傳說中的神奇動物，是天上的星星散開而生成，有祥瑞的象徵。民間相信麒麟送子來，此圖像代表「早生貴子，子孫賢德」的祝頌之意，傳說中孔子就是麒麟所送。在民間藝術中，一童子騎在麒麟背上，行於彩雲之間，手持一蓮花，代表「連生貴子」。

在＃51的圖案中，童子騎在麒麟身上，右手執蓮，左手捧笙，就是「連生貴子」的意思。我們可以見到作者把麒麟身上的鱗片，以及長鬚和尾部表現地非常精細，細緻的繡工和豐富的想像力，值得細細欣賞。

The *Qi lin*

The *qi lin* is an auspicious, mythical creature, originating from the scattered stars in the heavens. According to folktale, the *qi lin* delivered mankind to earth as depicted in this image. It also wishes the wearer lots of children and grandchildren in the future. (Figure 51)

子供を運んでくれる麒麟—麒麟送子

麒麟は伝説上の動物で、星より生まれたと言われていました。民間では「子供を運んでくれる」縁起のいい動物として崇めていました。民間芸術の中で、手に蓮の花を持っている男の子が麒麟の背中に乗り、雲の間を行き来する文様は「連生貴子」、つまり「子供が次々と生まれる」ことを意味しています。

#51は、まさにそのような文様です。麒麟の鱗や、長いヒゲ、尻尾などは大変よく出来ており、高度な技法と豊富な想像力が伺えます。

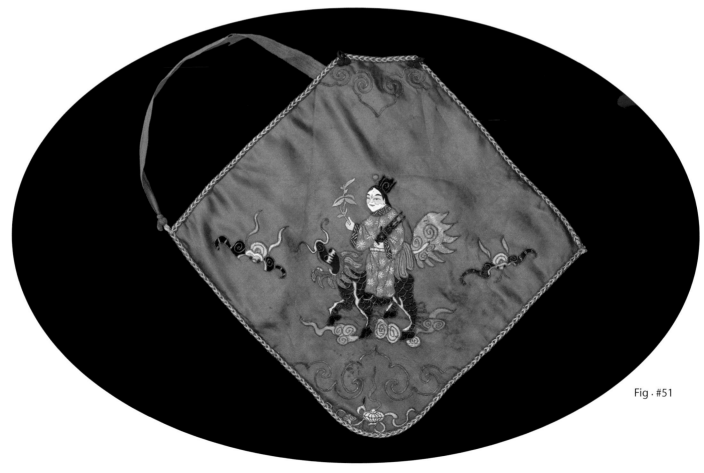

Fig．#51

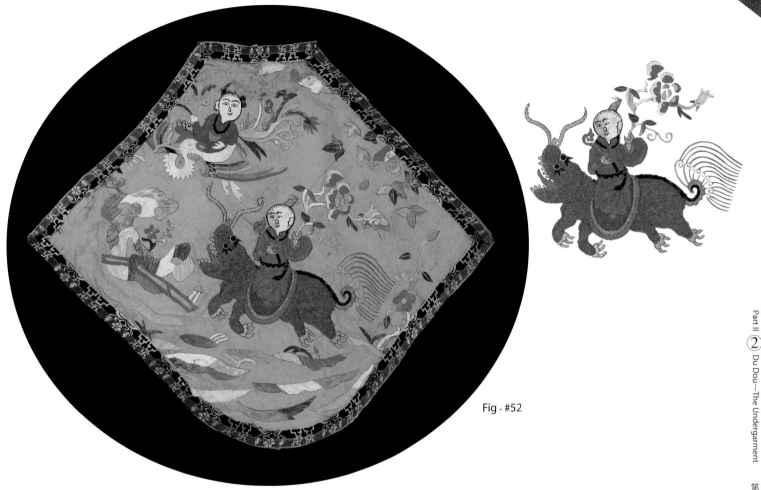

Fig . #52

⑤②
天仙送子

＃52這只肚兜是由山西一帶的婦女所縫製，作者綜合運用了打籽繡、破絲繡及細緻的萬字紋滾邊，加上豐富的人像與景物圖案，將這只肚兜妝點得熱鬧非凡。

肚兜中央為一騎在綠色麒麟背上的童子，童子右手拿如意，左手捧著花枝，上方似乎為騎在白鶴身上的天仙，手中也持象徵吉祥的靈芝。

值得注意的是畫面左方出現的太湖石，亦稱「洞庭石」，此類太湖石特別著重造型之美，講究的是「透、瘦、皺、漏」，暗含了中國人對生活理想和藝術追求的平和、穩定與嫻靜，一般在國畫山水的勾欄邊較常出現，在肚兜上則是較為罕見的圖飾，不妨多加欣賞。

The Fairy Sends Baby

This piece (Figure 52) is from the Shanxi region. In the center, we see that a young child is riding on a *qi lin*. In his right hand, he holds a *ru-yi*, and in his left, he is holding a flower branch. Above him is a fairy on a white crane, who is holding the auspicious *ling zhi*. According to legend, both the *qi lin* and the fairy bring children to couples who are praying for a baby.

子供を運んでくれる仙人—天仙送子

#52は山西辺りに住む女性の作品で、ノット．ステッチ、スプリット．シルク．ステッチなど、様々な難しい技法と多彩な飾りにより、一枚の絵を賑やかに表現しています。

注目するべきところは、左にある「太湖石」と呼ばれる石です。「太湖」という大きい湖から引き上げた石で、とても奇妙な形をしていて実に味わい深いものです。庭園を飾る石として昔から珍重され、古い山水画にもたびたび登場しています。腹掛けでは余り見かけない飾りなので、大変面白く価値のあるものだと思います。

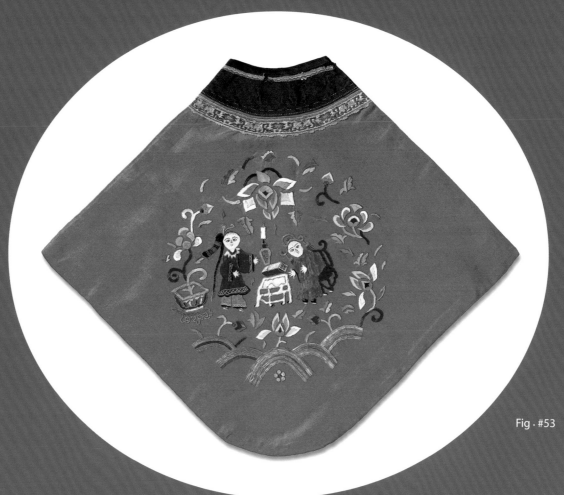

Fig．#53

㊼

洞房花燭夜

人生最快樂的事，莫過於「洞房花燭夜」，和「金榜題名時」，#53是收集自山西一帶的肚兜作品，上面繡的即是人生最美好的洞房花燭夜。美好的愛情以洞房花燭夜做為人生的另一個起點，想想看，真是讓人喜上眉梢。這只圍兜以鮮紅為底，繡上穿著整齊的新郎和身著鳳冠霞被的新嫁娘，兩人一站一坐，桌上則點著大大的喜燭，此情此景，是不是也讓你感染了濃濃的喜氣呢？

The Newlyweds' First Night

Perhaps the happiest night of one's life is the wedding night. Figure 53 comes from the Shanxi area and it depicts a couple's first night in their bedroom as a married couple, accompanied by the soft light of a candle. One person sits as the other stands—the excitement is almost palpable!

新婚初夜—洞房花燭夜

人生で一番楽しい時は、「洞房花燭夜」――「新婚初夜」及び「試験合格した時」とされています。#53は、山西から集めた腹掛けて、新婚初夜という人生最高と言われる場面が刺繍されています。愛する人との人生の新しい出発点に立つことは、なにより嬉しいことでしょう。鮮やかな赤の生地に、華麗に着飾った新郎新婦と、テーブルの上には大きなキャンドルが燃えています。こちらにまで漂ってきそうなほどの甘いムードのある作品です。

花團錦簇

Chapter 5　A Conglomeration of Splendid and Beautiful Things

第五章　咲き誇る花

54

花團錦簇之一

＃54是中國北方的作品。這件肚兜十分與眾不同，細心的母親用了成人的衣片拼湊成這件孩兒的肚兜，成人衣片上原來就有的各式刺繡紋飾，包括梅花和楓葉，將這件肚兜妝點得格外繽紛與花團錦簇。此外，母親另外還繡上了金線的雲紋，並為肚兜加上了盤長緞帶，感覺既美麗又有創意。

A Conglomeration of Splendid and Beautiful Things (1)

Figure 54 comes from northern China. It is an especially unique and different piece. This mother patched together fabrics from adult clothing to make a child's undergarment. In the adjoining strip of fabric, she has stitched all kinds of floral patterns. This is a very creative piece.

咲き誇る花その1

「花團錦簇」は綺麗な花が咲き乱れている様子をいいます。#54は中国の北方から収集したもので、作り方はほかの作品と大分違っています。これは大人服の布切れを継ぎはぎして作ったため、元々あった梅や楓の刺繡などの飾りがそのまま残っており、色とりどりで華やかな感じがする一点です。このほか、金の糸で雲の文様を刺繡したり、盤長結び文様の縁取りが施されていたりするなどの工夫も見られます。

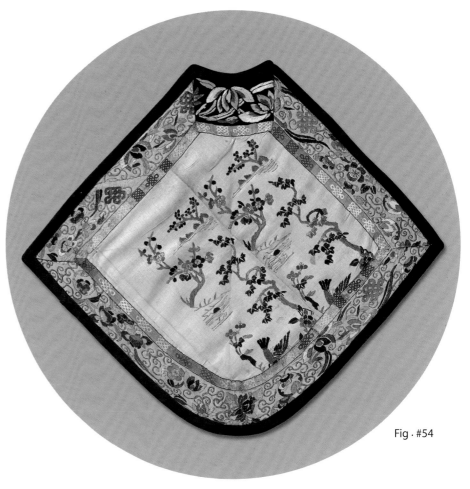

Fig．#54

55

花團錦簇之二

同樣是是以花為主題，#55這件肚兜不一樣的地方，是採用了貼布的手法，創造出層疊的立體感，暗色的布面，襯上鮮豔繡線繡出的斗大花朵，顯得十分搶眼。此肚兜為浙江寧波一帶的作品。

A Conglomeration of Splendid and Beautiful Things (2)

Although Figure 55 also uses flowers as its subject, the difference is apparent here in technique—here the appliqué technique is used for a lively, three-dimensional effect. The result is very eye-catching. This undergarment is from the area around Ningbo.

咲き誇る花その2

同じように花を主題としたものですが、浙江寧波から収集した#55の腹掛けは、暗色の生地に鮮やかな糸で大輪の花を描き、見る人の視線を釘付けにします。見所は花に施したアップリケ技法です。これにより、花はくっきりとした立体感があり生き生きとしています。

Fig・#55

吉獸報喜　Chapter 6　Auspicious Animals Sending Good Tidings
第六章 喜びを知らせる吉祥動物

(56)

青獅

獅子雖非中國原有的動物，但中國確有自屬的「獅文化」，以獅子為驅邪避崇的吉物。各宮殿衙門，還有大戶人家門外兩旁大多擺置獅子，除鎮宅驅邪外，因獅子凶猛威嚴，因此也成了權威的象徵。

此外，獅子與「師」同音，在官府門前左邊大獅子為「太師」，這是朝廷中最高的官階，右邊的獅子代表「少保」，是王子的侍衛，所以，獅子也有用來祝人官運亨通，飛黃騰達之意。

＃56是一件相當能代表青獅在中國吉祥象徵的肚兜，縫製這件肚兜的媽媽，用了相當技巧來表現青獅的活靈活現，看肚兜中央的青獅抬著頭、舉起右前爪，模樣神氣十足。在青獅後方的是典型的太湖石，周遭還環繞了樹木、花朵與飛舞的蟲鳥，使整件肚兜顯得相當豐富。

The Green Lion

As mentioned earlier, although lions did not originate from China, there is a distinct Chinese "lion's culture," which uses the lion as a symbol of power and a means to ward off evil. One will often see a pair of lions at the gate of a palace or in front of a wealthy home. In addition, because the pronunciation of "lion" (shi) in Chinese is the same as that of "teacher" or "official," lions in front of a governmental building also represent the highest official ranking.

Figure 56 is a perfect representation of the green lion as an auspicious symbol in Chinese culture. The lion in the center of the undergarment is looking upwards, with its right paw raised; he looks very lively and full of energy. Behind the lion is a typical rendering of the Tai-Lake rock and surrounding them are trees, flowers, and flying insects and birds, making this design very abundant and full of life.

魔よけの青獅

中国に獅子はいませんが、独特の獅子文化を持っており、魔よけや厄払いのための縁起物として愛されてきました。昔の宮殿や官庁、あるいは上流階級の屋敷の玄関で、いつも獅子は鎮座していました。またその猛猛しい姿から「権威」の象徴にもなったのです。

獅子は「師」と同音のため、官庁の玄関に置かれている獅子の向かって左の方は「太師」と呼ばれ、朝廷で最高の官位に当ります。右の獅子は「少保」といい、王子の護衛に当ります。そのため、獅子は「出世」を意味する場合もあります。

＃56は獅子のめでたい意味を存分に表しているものです。真ん中の青い獅子は、頭を擡げて右手を上げ威張っています。後ろに太湖石があり、回りには木や、花、蝶など、賑やかな図柄になっています。

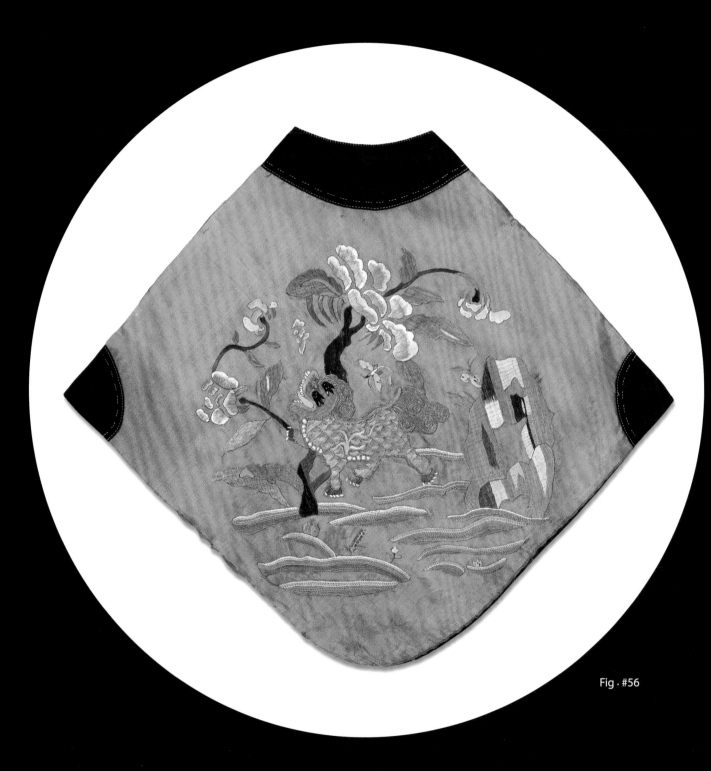

Fig . #56

57

獅子戲球

「獅子戲球」又稱「獅子戲繡球」，在民間的遊藝活動中時常可見，與古代僧人法事的「獅子會」或「太師少保」應該有聯繫的關係。

＃57是收集自山西一帶的孩兒肚兜，黑底襯紅的用色加上特殊的挖雲貼布技法，顯得相當出色，其上繡的圖案也是繽紛五彩。

在肚兜下方可以見到「獅子戲球」，獅子微張的嘴和傘狀散開的尾巴，加上腹下的粉紅色繡球，顯得生動又俏皮。在肚兜上方及兩側，則散佈了石榴、盤長、壽字紋、佛手與喜鵲，為肚兜更添加了洋洋喜氣。

Fig . #57

The Lion Playing with a Ball

Figure 57 was collected from Shanxi. On the bottom of the undergarment, there is a lion with an eager, open mouth and an umbrella-like tail that is fanned out behind him. The colorful ball he is playing with is beneath him. On either side of the undergarment, there are embroideries of pomegranates, characters for longevity, and Buddha's hands, all of which add to the festive and playful subject of this design. The lion playing with a ball is a symbol of joy.

ボールで遊ぶ獅子—獅子戲球

「獅子戲球」──人が演じている獅子がボールで遊んでいる姿は、よく民間の祭りで見かけます。＃57は山西から収集した腹掛けで、黒の生地に赤い色を使い、陶磁器の技法の「赤地掻き落し」のような効果を出しています。また色鮮やかな様々な文様は、大変美しいものです。

絵柄の下の方に、獅子がボールで遊んでいる姿が見られます。微かに開けた口、傘のように広がった尻尾、お腹の下にある桃色のボールなど、可愛さいっぱいの構図になっています。絵の上と両側に石榴、盤長結び、「寿」字紋、仏の手、カササギなどもあり、一層めでたい感じがします。

鶴

＃58是一件繡工精緻，十分值得細細欣賞的刺繡佳作。肚兜中央繡的仙鶴，一腳站立，雙翅開展，同時回頭頻看，將仙鶴的靈巧表現的非常生動，而以金色絲線滾邊也凸顯了華麗的質感。

鶴是一品鳥，自古就與仙人道士雲遊，地位僅次於鳳凰。這只肚兜上的仙鶴，站立在潮頭岩石，寓意「一品當朝」。此外，仙鶴也是長壽的代表，相傳只有鶴找得到靈芝，而且懂得守護靈芝，因此也與長壽有關。

長生きと出世の象徵—鶴

＃58は大変力のこもった作品で、時間を掛けてじっくり楽しむに値する作品でしょう。中央の鶴が一本足で立ち、二つの羽根を広げながら振り返る様は、鶴ならではの優雅な姿を現しています。また金の糸を使ったことで華やかさも感じられます。

中国で鶴は、鳳凰に次ぐ地位の高い鳥とされ、昔から仙人に伴って四方に旅する鳥だと信じられていました。また「水辺の岩場に佇む一羽の鶴」は、「一品（鶴の別名）當潮（水辺に居る）」として、「出世」を意味しています。さらに、鶴だけが、長生きの霊薬、「さるのこしかけ」を見つけ、守ることが出来ると言われていますので、「長生き」の象徴でもあります。

The Crane: **A Symbol for Longevity and the First Rank Civil Officer**

The crane is a celebrated bird in Chinese legend and has many mythical attributes. As a symbol, it is often shown with lifted foot and spread-out wings—as such, it is one of the most common symbols of longevity. The crane also represents civil officers of the first rank. The crane often accompanies divinity or immortals wandering about in nature. The crane in Figure 58 is embroidered in majestic detail. The gold threads that create the border of the undergarment make it look especially spectacular.

Fig . #58

望子成龍

Chapter 7 To Hope One's Children Will Have a Bright Future

第七章 光明吉祥の象徵－太陽

㊾

指日高陞

＃59這件來自中國北方的肚兜，以對孩子未來的祝福，表現母親對孩兒的愛心與深切期望。

肚兜中央可見一名頭戴官帽的官人，站在高崗上，表示「孩子成人了」，一手舉向天空，似乎指著天上高懸的太陽，一旁繡以「指日高陞」，引出了此幅圖的典故，希望孩兒長大成人、步步高陞。「指日高陞」與「狀元誇官」意同。在官人身旁的是盛開的牡丹花，而肚兜頸項處，有回字紋緞帶作為裝飾。

Promotion Can Be Expected Very Soon

This piece is from northern China. In Figure 59,the center of the undergarment is a Figure wearing the hat of an official. He is standing on a mountain top, which symbolizes adulthood. The figure has a raised hand, perhaps pointing to the sun, and the phrase "point to the sun and rise up" is embroidered next to him. The significance of this design is revealed through these words. The mother hopes that her child will become an adult and rise up through the ranks of society very soon.

いつの日か必ず出世する—指日高昇

＃59は、中国の北方から収集したもので、母親の我が子に対する期待が伺える作品です。中央に官吏の帽子を被った役人風の男性が、小高い山の頂に立ち、空に懸かっている太陽を指差しています。これは「指日高昇」、つまり

「いつか必ず出世する」ことを意味しています。めでたい牡丹の花や回字紋も飾られています。

Fig．#59

第
貳
部

兜
兜
情
事
—
肚
兜

⑥⓪

五毒

五毒又稱「五毒符」，繪有蜈蚣、蜥蜴、蠍子、蛇、蛙等五種動物，以刺繡貼布方式做成肚兜等物，配在兒童身上，可以除魔避邪，特別是端午節，初夏時分，毒蟲叢生，多以五毒掛身以避之。在＃60-1和＃60-2的孩兒肚兜上，都可明顯看到五毒的驅邪避疫圖案。

The Five Poisons

The Five Poisons are the viper, the scorpion, the centipede, the toad, and the spider. When embroidered onto children's clothing, they are meant to ward off evil, especially during the Dragon Boat Festival, which falls on the fifth day of the fifth lunar month when poisonous insects become very active. In both Figure 60-1 and Figure 60-2, you can clearly see the depictions of the five poisonous creatures.

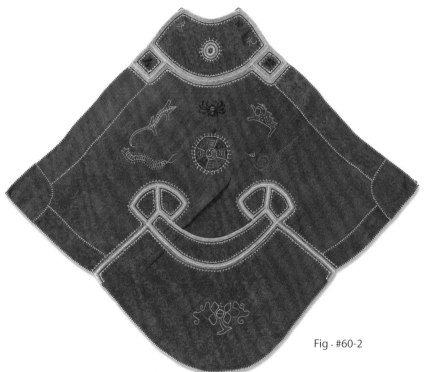

Fig・#60-2

魔よけのお札—五毒

「五毒」は、百足、蜥蜴、蠍、蛇、蛙を指しており、この5つの動物の文様を描いたものは、「魔除けのお札」ともいいます。この動物の刺繡とアップリケで腹掛けを作り、子供に着せると魔除けの効果が得られると信じられました。特に端午の節句の時期は、ちょうど初夏に当るので、毒のある虫が至るところで発生するため、人々は五毒のお札をお守りとして身につける習慣がありました。#60-1も、#60-2も、五毒の文様が見られます。

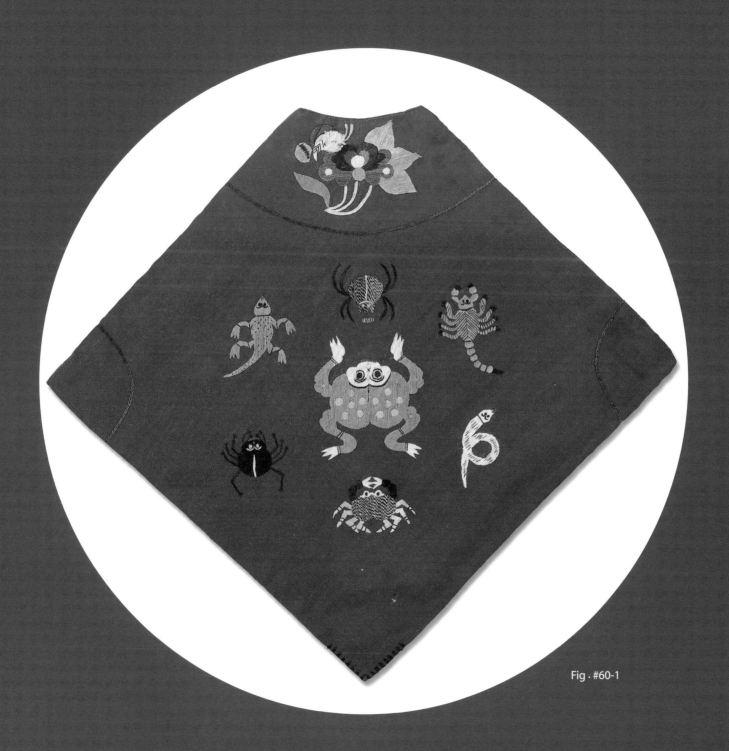

Fig·#60-1

第玖章

成人肚兜 Chapter 9 Undergarments *(Du Duo)* for Adults
第九章 大人の腹掛け

(61)

客家肚兜

#61是屬於台灣客家女性的肚兜，淡綠的色澤，顯得相當典雅，在刺繡的表現上則相當出色，可以細細欣賞。一般來說，孩童的肚兜多使用貼布等技法，但成人的肚兜，多專注在刺繡的表現，這只肚兜繡上了許多花卉和藤蔓等美麗的圖形，中間下方有隻展翅的蝴蝶，整體風格顯得極為秀麗雅致。

Undergarments for Adults

Figure 61 is an undergarment that a young Taiwanese Hakka woman would wear. Its pale green color is very elegant, as is the delicate embroidery. As a very general rule the embroidery for adult clothing is much more refined and complex.

客家人の腹掛け

#61は、台湾の客家女性による大人用の腹掛けです。淡い緑の色は大変典雅な感じを与えています。刺繍もすばらしくじっくりと楽しめる一点です。一般的に、子供用の腹掛けはアップリケの技法をよく使いますが、大人用は、刺繍が中心です。この腹掛けには、花や蔓等の綺麗な飾りがふんだんに取り入れられ、中央下には羽根を広げた蝶がいて、雅やかで麗しいものです。

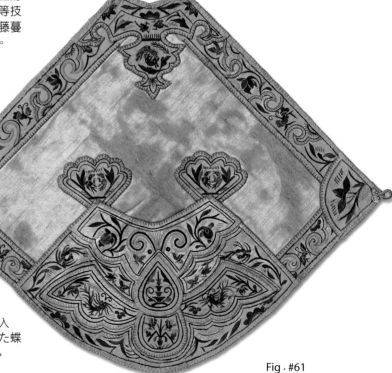

Fig · #61

Fig . #62

⑥② 春耕圖

#62可能也是成年婦女的肚兜用品，這件肚兜以黑色為底，繡以五彩繡線，在紋飾方面，可以看到創作者首先以綠色的繡線，勾勒出簡單雅致的圖形變化；在肚兜下方中央，則有人趕驢的圖樣，是民間常見的春耕圖，代表婦女祈求風調雨順、五穀豐收的吉祥意涵，另外還有吉慶富貴的鳳鳥圖案。

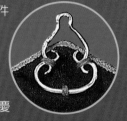

另外，這只肚兜在上方的頸項處，使用了葫蘆形狀的金色扣子，金光燦爛，為這只肚兜增添了幾許華麗與別緻之感。

Spring

This undergarment is also very likely for a young lady. The scene depicted on the bottom of Figure 62 is that of a farmer plowing the field during spring harvest time. This means the woman wearing this undergarment was hoping for a successful and bountiful harvest. Notice the delicate buttons at the neck of the undergarment—they give the piece a subtle touch of style.

春耕の場面―春耕図

#62は大人用と思われます。黒の生地に、色鮮やかな糸で刺繍しています。緑の糸でシンプルですが品よく変化に富んだ線が描かれ、下の方には、驢馬(ロバ)と歩いている男性がいます。これは民間でよく見かける「春耕図」、つまり「春先田んぼで耕している」場面です。その下には、めでたい鳳凰がいます。「豊富な収穫があるように」という女性からの祈りが込められています。

また、首周りのところに、珍しい瓢箪の形をした綺麗な金のボタンが付けられており、この腹掛けに華やかさを添えています。

63

梅花鹿

＃63是一只非常美麗的肚兜，收集自山西一帶，肚兜中央是口吐靈芝的梅花鹿，象徵吉祥長壽，兩側有如意雲紋，上方的頸項處則飾以扇形，也有文人手持繡扇、文采風流的寓意。創作者以精細的挖雲技法，在肚兜的下方繡以美麗的蓮花和金魚，有文人愛蓮之意，也可視為金魚戲蓮的夫妻恩愛之情。

長生きの象徴─梅花鹿

＃63は大変華麗な腹掛けで、山西の辺りから収集してきました。中央に、「さるのこしかけ」の草を銜えた鹿がいて、これは「長生き」を意味する縁起物です。また両側に「如意雲」の文様が飾られ、さらに上の方には、扇子の形の飾りが施されています。扇子は「文人」のイメージがするので、文才風流の意味があります。さらに一番下には、オープン．ワーク．エンブロイダリーという技法で、一対の金魚と蓮の葉が飾られ、「文人は蓮の花を愛する」という意味が込められています。また金魚と蓮の組み合わせは「夫婦円満」の象徴でもあります。

Deer with White Spots

Figure 63 shows a beautiful undergarment from the Shanxi area. In the center is a deer spitting out *ling zhi* (a kind of fungus which is supposed to possess supernatural powers) from its mouth, which symbolizes longevity. On either side are *ru-yi* clouds. Around the neck opening is a fan-like design, which recalls the fans used by scholars. On the bottom of the undergarment are lotus flowers and goldfish, which symbolize the love between a woman and her husband.

Fig．#63

第貳部 兜兜情事─肚兜

64

蓮

＃64的肚兜整件都是以管狀琉璃做
成，肚兜面上分佈了蓮花、蓮蓬與蓮
葉等美麗的圖飾。這件作品上的蓮花
以粉紅、藍、與綠色的管狀琉璃裝
飾，除了花朵嬌豔，整件肚兜都閃爍
著琉璃的迷人光彩，蓮子並以銅鏡裝
飾，做工非常精美，是很特殊的一個
設計。

蓮在百花之中，有「花中君子」之
稱，因出淤泥而不染，也有「一品清
廉（蓮）」之意。另外蓮蓬多子，也
帶有多子多孫與綿延不斷的寓意。

The Lotus: Purity

This piece is made of tubular antique
glass. It is embroidered with images
of lotus flowers, lotus leaves, and lotus
cupules. The pink, blue, and green glass
pieces on this piece are mesmerizing,
and the needlework is especially
delicate, while the design itself is
unique. The lotus plant emerges out
of the mud, and yet it looks as clean
and pure as though it had never been
touched by dirt. The lotus is admired
for its purity. (Figure 64)

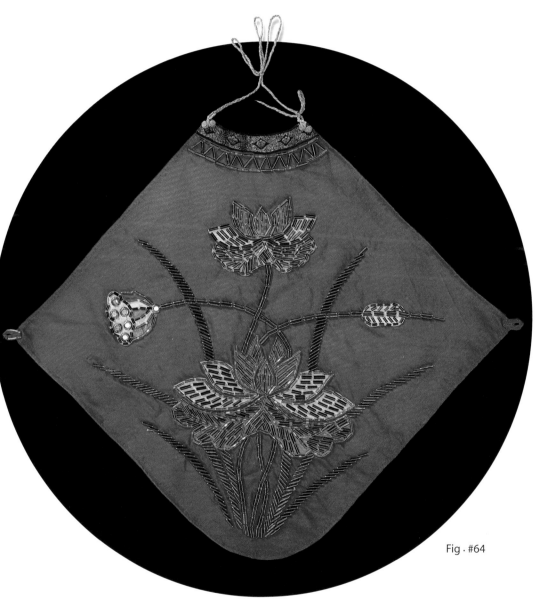

Fig . #64

美しい蓮

#64の腹掛けには、蓮の花、蓮の花托、蓮の葉などが美しく飾られ、これらはすべて瑠
璃でできた細い管を繋ぎ合わせ、生地に縫いつけたものです。瑠璃を材料としたため、
全体がきらきらと光り、また花托の中の蓮の子には小さな銅鏡を嵌めこんでいるので輝
いています。この腹掛けは、全体として大変精緻で独特なデザインと言えましょう。

第 ③ 部 造型特殊的圍兜

Part III --- **Special Bibs**

第三部 --- 独特な形の涎掛け

第 壹 章

爭奇鬥豔 Chapter 1　To Contend in beauty and fascination

第一章 奇をてらし、艶を競う

⑥⑤

有鳳來儀

圍兜是寶寶的生活用品，但在婦女的細心巧思與創意下，有些圍兜以相當特殊的造型出現，表露出獨具一格的藝術美感，相當難能可貴。像#65這只類似鳳鳥造型的圍兜，已經是令人激賞的藝術品了。

鳳凰為鳥中之王，雄曰鳳，雌曰凰，屬仁德之鳥。傳說中鳳有大鵬的翅膀，仙鶴的腿，鸚鵡的嘴，孔雀的尾，是美好與和平的象徵，也是吉祥與喜氣的代表。在古代，鳳是皇后的代表，與帝王的象徵－－龍，互為匹配。

#65的圍兜，整件就是一隻鳳鳥的造型，縫製這只圍兜的婦女以圈金的方式，把鳳鳥的頭、翼、尾細膩地刻畫出來，並利用貼布技法，將不同色澤的布片組成鳳的羽翼，五彩斑斕。這名聰明的婦女，另外還將鳳鳥的頭部設計成桃子的造型，尾部則像散開的石榴，讓這只圍兜更添吉祥如意的意味。

鳳凰飛来－有鳳来儀

涎掛けは日常生活の実用品ですが、母親の創意工夫により、相当変化のある形の作品も見かけます。次に登場するこれらの涎掛けは、一味違う芸術的な魅力を持っている、大変珍しい作品です。

#65の作品は、鳳凰のような形をしていて、眼を見張るような出来栄えです。鳥の頭、翼、尻尾などの輪郭を縁取りで描き、色の違う生地によるアップリケで色鮮やかな翼を組み合わせました。作者は大変鋭い感性の持ち主と見え、鳥の頭部を桃に、尻尾を広がる石榴にイメージすることにより、めでたい感じをより一段と出しました。

Phoenix Brings Prosperity

Though the baby's bib is an item for everyday use, through the creativity and careful design of certain mothers, some bibs have been elevated to actual works of art. Such is the case of the bib in Figure 65 that is itself shaped like a phoenix.

According to legend, the phoenix had the wings of a big roc, the legs of a crane, the beak of a mandarin duck, and the tail of a peacock, and it is the emblem of beauty, peace, and fortune. The phoenix is also the symbol of the empress, next to the dragon, who is the symbol of the emperor.

The maker of this phoenix bib is quite creative and clever— not only is the bib in the shape of a phoenix, with different colored fabric layered upon each other to form the multi-layers of the phoenix's wings, she also made the head of the phoenix into the shape of the peach (symbol of longevity), and the tail into the shape of a pomegranate (symbol of life and reproduction.)

Fig . #65

66

桃形圍兜

#66是一只桃形圍兜，除了造型特殊，圍兜雙面上也繡有非常精緻的人物圖樣，並在三個側邊飾以美麗的流蘇長穗。

在圍兜的一邊，可以看見一名官人站立，旁有兩名手拿旗子的童子，天空中有「日」、「月」雲飾。這是民間流傳「狀元誇官」的故事，「誇官」是指狀元高中後，皇帝特令其拿旗披彩、乘騎遊街誇耀的故事。圍兜另一邊所繡的是「麒麟送子」，這和「狀元誇官」是一系列中的圖案，新婚吉祥賀語，意謂可生貴子，更可成大器。天上的太陽，有「丹鳳朝陽」之意。

桃形の涎掛け

#66は、両面刺繍の涎掛けで、桃の形をしています。形が珍しいほか、刺繍された人物が非常に細やかで、また房飾りが三箇所付けられています。左の文様は、昔のある男性の「大出世」にまつわる「状元誇官」という民間話に基づくものです。右の方は「麒麟送子」という「早く子供が生まれますように」という願いが込められる文様です。いずれも新婚に相応しい祝福の言葉です。

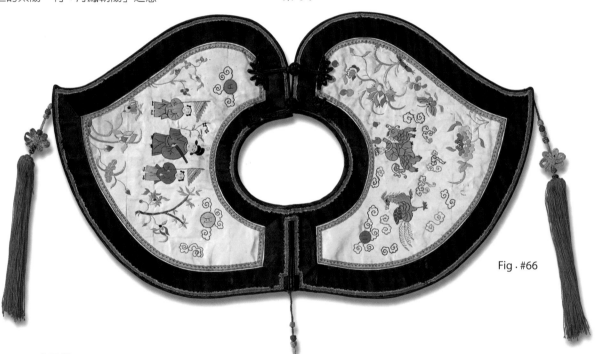

Fig・#66

Peach-shaped Bib

This is a peach-shaped bib. Aside from its unique design, the embroidery on both sides includes very intricate renderings of human figures and features beautiful tassel decorations on the three sides.

On one side of the bib (Figure 66), there is an official standing in the center with two children on either side of him, holding up flags. In the sky are two clouds with the characters for "sun" and "moon" embroidered on them. This depicts the famous folk tale of a top candidate for the imperial examination being paraded on the streets to show off his achievements. On the other side of the bib is the story of the *qi lin* delivering mankind to earth.

第參部 造型特殊的圍兜

Fig . #67

67

蝶形圍兜

好一隻美麗的蝴蝶！把＃67的圍兜撲展開來，就是一隻翩翩起舞的蝴蝶。

創作者除了細心裁剪出蝴蝶美麗的雙翅，還用心塑造了蝴蝶的頭部和尾部，蝴蝶的頭部頗似人形，另採用堆疊的手法在眼部做出立體感，十分可愛。在蝴蝶的紅色雙翅上，是極細的鎖繡繡出的花紋與藤蔓，看得出創作者富有極美麗的心思。

蝶形の涎掛け

#67は、眼が醒めるような美しい蝶です。綺麗な羽根もさることながら、人間に似た頭の形も、そして尻尾も大層な工夫が見られます。さらに重ねる手法により、可愛い眼に立体感を持たせました。両方の羽根にある花や蔓は、ゴールド．エンブロイダリーという特殊な刺繍によるもので、作者の巧みな創意が伺えます。

Butterfly-shaped Bib

What a beautiful butterfly! Once you spread out the bib in Figure 67, it becomes a butterfly just about to take off. The head of the butterfly is anthropomorphic, with an expression much like a human's. The eyes were made by using the relief technique to give it a three-dimensional effect. On the wings of the butterfly are curlicues of flowers and flower stems that make the piece that much more exquisite.

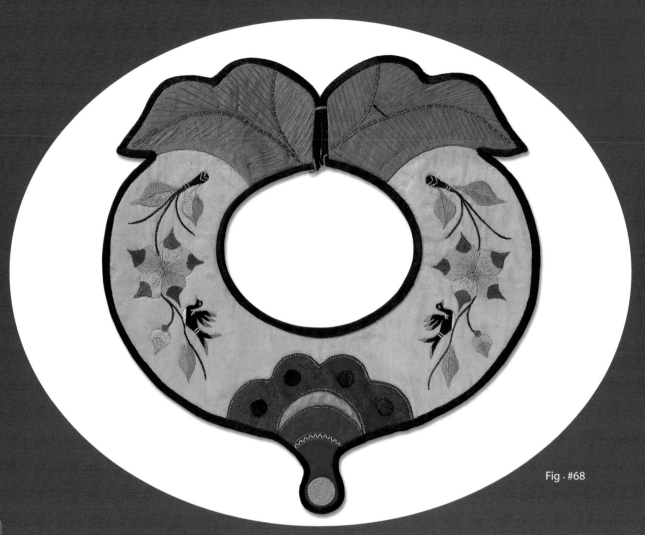

Fig · #68

68

果形圍兜

翠綠的葉片，加上豐盈飽滿的果實，＃68是一只果實形狀、特殊造型的圍兜。創作者在葉片上以金蔥繡出條理分明的脈絡，果實狀的圍兜面上則繡上粉紅的花朵。不知道寶寶使用這只圍兜時，是不是也會時時嗅到果實濃郁飽滿的香氣呢？

果物の形の涎掛け

＃68は、緑色の葉と、丸々として美味しそうな果物とで形作られました。葉には、タッセル（Tassels）という技法で、金の糸でくっきりとした葉脈が刺繡され、果物には桃色の花が飾られました。子供がこの涎掛けを掛けたら、瑞々しい果物の香りが漂ってくるようです。

Fruit-shaped Bib

Figure 68 is a fruit-shaped bib—its jade green leaves and full, ripe shape make it look almost delectable. With the delicate, pink flowers embroidered on either side, one wonders whether the baby wearing this bib can smell whiffs of sweetness from the fruit.

裝飾性強的圍兜 Chapter 2 Bibs with Accessories
第二章 装飾的な涎掛け

⑥⑨

美麗的流蘇之一

長長的流蘇，和圍兜上美麗的刺繡與配色，＃69這只圍兜，第一眼就緊緊吸引人的目光，叫人忍不住發出：「好美！」的讚嘆。

儘管圍兜大多屬於孩兒日常用品，有些富貴人家或具有特殊美感的母親，還是用心地把孩兒圍兜縫製的美輪美奐，並加上裝飾性強的一些飾物，在正式場合裡，讓孩兒也可以打扮得一身美麗又喜氣。

＃69在圍兜的八個葉片上，分別使用了四條長形的流蘇，搭配四條繫有長繩的銅鈴，孩兒蹦蹦跳跳時，發出清脆的鈴聲，既有裝飾效果又十分地悅耳。圍兜面以絲緞製成，紫與黑的搭配相當美麗出色，上面並繡有盤長、花卉與如意雲頭的吉祥紋飾。

美しい房飾りその1

この涎掛けの長い房飾りと見事な色使いを眼にしたら人々は思わず感嘆の声をあげてしまうことでしょう。涎掛けは日常品でも、裕福な家や美的センスを持っている母親は、やはり工夫を惜しみません。見栄えのする涎掛けは、晴れの場でも、子供の立派な飾りになると思います。

#69には、4本の長い房飾りと、4本の先端に銅の鈴が付いた紐がついています。子供が動くと、鈴は鳴り、大変可愛らしいものです。生地は紫と黒のシルクで作られ、配色は大変垢抜けていて、その上に盤長結び、花、如意雲などのめでたい文様が刺繍されています。

Fig . #69

Beautiful Tassels (1)

The long tassels and beautiful colors and embroidery on this bib attract one's attention immediately. It makes you want to exclaim "How gorgeous!"

Though the bib is something the baby uses everyday for very practical purposes, sometimes mothers from a more wealthy background, or those who have an eye for the decorative, will accessorize their babies' bibs so that they can be worn on special occasions.

On the eight petals of Figure 69, the mother attached four long tassels and four ribbons with bells on the ends so that when the baby moves about, there will be the crisp sounds of bells chiming. Notice the flower and cloud motifs on the bib, both of which are auspicious symbols that bring the baby good fortune.

⑦⓪

美麗的流蘇之二

五角的特殊造型，加上五串長長的流蘇，＃70的圍兜也是屬於裝飾性十分強的美麗衣飾。

這只圍兜的刺繡也非常精緻。在頸項處，使用了貼布繡的手法繡出十個如意雲紋，並以金蔥框出輪廓，繡工綿密且立體感十足。而在五角形的圍兜面上，另外繡上了熱鬧的人物與花鳥，可以看見兩人中間立有一隻獅子，而在圍兜背部中央有個藍色繡線的壽字。這只圍兜整體看來，流露出一股難以抵擋的華麗與貴氣。

Beautiful Tassels (2)

This pentagonal bib with five long tassels is also very unique, with a strong design. Around the collar of the bib, using the appliqué method, the mother has stitched ten *ru-yi* cloud motifs. In Figure 70, she has embroidered figures of people, flowers, and birds. Between the two people there is a lion, and at the top of the pentagon (where the bib would lie on the baby's back) there is the character for longevity *(shou)* stitched with blue thread. With all its details, this bib looks especially ornate.

Fig · #70

美しい房飾りその2

#70は珍しい五角形である上、長い房飾りが付けられ、装飾性の強い一点です。首周りにアップリケで10の如意雲を刺繍し、さらにタッセル細工で縁取りをしました。いずれも立体感を十分持っている見事な出来具合であります。その周りには人物と花と鳥が賑やかに飾られ、二人の人の間に獅子が一頭いて、裏面の中央に青い「寿」の字が刺繍されています。大変贅沢感のある涎掛けと言えましょう。

美麗的流蘇之三

流線型的荷葉邊,加上流蘇,#71這只圍兜,線條顯得非常流暢與柔和。

仔細欣賞圍兜上的刺繡,作者在葉子和鳥的部分,使用了特別的別絨繡法,在花朵部分則使用華麗的格錦繡法,此外以盤金方式,將面上的荷花與荷葉點綴的十分華美。此外,面上繡有鸚鵡與石榴、佛手與仙桃。「石榴、佛手、仙桃」又稱為「三多」,有「多福、多壽、多子」的吉祥意味。

Beautiful Tassels (3)

The flowing curvature of this bib (Figure 71) recalls the fluid outlines of a lotus leaf. Upon close examination, we see that the maker of this bib used one technique to embroider the leaves and the birds and another to embroider the flowers. This bib has the "three plenties"—plenty of fortune, plenty of life, and plenty of children, symbolized, respectively, by the Buddha's hand, the peach, and the pomegranate.

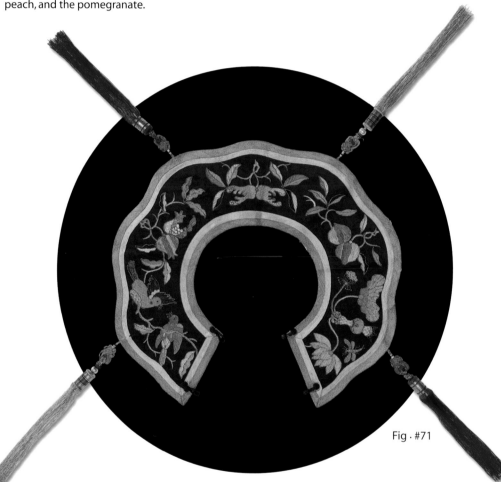

Fig . #71

美しい房飾りその3

流れるような縁の線と房飾りが、#71の涎掛けに流暢で柔和な感じをもたらしています。よく見ると、葉と鳥の部分にペーブ．ステッチ(Pave stitch)に似た特別な刺繡法が取り入れられており、花の部分では、華やかさをそえるためのブロケード．エンブロイダリー(Brocade embroidery)という技法が採られています。更に蓮の花と葉はゴールド．エンブロイダリーという技法で、きらびやかに仕上がっています。そのほか石榴、仏の手、桃があり、この3つの果物の組み合わせは「三多」とも呼ばれ、「多福、多寿、多子」、つまり裕福、長生き、子孫繁栄の意味を持っています。

華美的圍兜之一

＃72的圍兜，在設計成花瓣狀的圍兜葉片上，繡上緊密的滾邊，相當醒目。

這件圍兜作品，在刺繡上表現的非常突出細緻，仔細看看，六個花瓣狀的葉片上，分別繡上的花卉與鳥，或飛，或站立，甚至擁有不同的表情與造型，栩栩如生，甚至有宮廷畫家畫作的細膩水準，值得細細品味欣賞。這裡的花卉與鳥，即是喜氣洋洋的「喜鵲登梅」。

Luxurious Bibs (1)

The panels of Figure 72 resemble petals of a flower. On each petal are embroideries of different birds and flowers. Whether the birds are in mid-flight, or standing still, they each have their own personality and expression. This bib is not only life-like, it is also full of life.

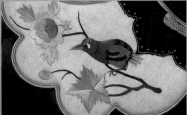

Fig . #72

華やかな涎掛けその1

#72は、花びら状の生地の上に、しっかりと縁取りが施され、非常に色鮮やかな涎掛けです。その刺繍は見事なもので、よく見ると、6つの花びら状の生地に、それぞれ花とカササギの文様が施されています。カササギは立っていたり、飛んでいたり、異なった仕草と形をし、今にも動き出しそうな生き生きとした感じがします。この絵は宮廷絵師の作品並みの水準を持っていると言ってよいほどの出来です。なお、カササギと梅の組み合わせは、非常にめでたい意味を持っています。

華美的圍兜之二

六隻蝴蝶翩翩飛舞！＃73這只孩兒圍兜，創作者在葉片部分設計出六隻蝴蝶圍成一圈的特殊造型，十分引人注目。

貼布手法在這只圍兜上被完美的運用著，一層接一層的不同顏色貼布，創造出層層疊疊又色彩繽紛的效果。仔細看，有粉紅、紅、綠、淺藍、深藍、嫩黃、紫等七種顏色，真是七彩奪目，令人目不暇給。

華やかな涎掛けその2

#73は、6つの蝶が艶やかに踊っていて、形として大変斬新なアイディアで人の目を惹きます。全体はアップリケの技法が駆使され、幾重にも重なり合う布切れは多彩さを極めています。よく見ると、桃色、赤、緑、水色、薄黄色、紫など7つの色があり、眼を見張るほど美しいものです。

Luxurious Bibs (2)

In Figure 73, six butterflies with overlapping wings, flying in unison! Using the appliqué method, each section of the wing overlaps another in a precise order, giving the piece a dizzyingly colorful effect. Notice the colors— pink, red, green, blue, indigo, yellow, and purple—the seven colors of a butterfly rainbow.

Fig . #73

華美的圍兜之三

#74是收集自安徽一帶的作品。
創作這只圍兜的婦女，利用如意
雲紋的變化創造出五個流線型的
葉片，上繡有捲曲的雲飾、細緻
的滾邊和花卉，另外，並以紅、
綠、藍、嫩黃與鮮黃等五個不同
的顏色來烘托。整件圍兜，看起
來就像一朵美麗的雲彩。

Luxurious Bibs (3)

Each petal of this bib (Figure 74)
has the fluid lines and shape of a
cloud motif. When all five petals
are stitched together, the entire
bib resembles a cloud shape.
Follow the curls of the lines and
there is movement to the bib.

Fig. #74

華やかな涎掛けその3

#74は安徽から収集した作品で、形は「如意雲」を上手く変化させた5つ
の、流れるようなラインを持つ葉からなっています。その上には精細な緣
取りのくるくるとくねる雲の飾りと、色とりどりの花があります。赤、
緑、青、薄黄色、明るい黄色などの配色により、全体は一片の綺麗な雲の
ように見えます。

Fig‧#75

75

華美的圍兜之四

#75是一件非常美麗的圍兜，上面綴有十九塊雕刻精緻的玉，以玉的狀況判斷這十九塊玉均屬古玉，年代已經相當久遠，這些古玉均由工匠巧雕，將來料雕成最適合的形體與花飾，裡頭不乏兩兩成對的雕飾，顯露出工匠精細的手工和品味。

這件圍兜繡有許多美麗的圖案，值得欣賞的是以金線繡成的鳳凰，繡工華美而精細，而圍兜邊上的如意雲紋，用色活潑，為這只圍兜增添幾許吉祥意味。

華やかな涎掛けその4

#75は非常に綺麗な涎掛けで、生地には精巧に細工された玉が19個も縫い付けられています。これらの玉は全て古いもので、17～19世紀の清の時代のものと思われます。いずれも玉材の元来の形状に沿って、もっともぴったりした形に彫られたもので、中には対になっているものもあります。この涎掛けは職人の高度な技とセンスが伺える優れたものです。また文樣が豊富で、注目するべき所は、金の糸で刺繍した華麗にして精緻な鳳凰であります。また緣の辺りの如意紋は、配色が大変鮮やかで、この涎掛けにめでたさを加えています。

Luxurious Bibs (4)

There are nineteen pieces of jade sewn onto this bib (Figure 75). These are the antique jade with delicate carvings. In addition to jade there are auspicious motifs such as the phoenix embroidered with gold thread, and the *ru-yi* cloud pattern decorating the edge of the bib.

第  章

方形的圍兜 Chapter 3 Square Bibs
第三章 四方形の涎掛け

⑦⑥

方形的趣味之一

#76是中國北方的圍兜作品，整件圍兜為方正的造型，以極細的鎖繡製成，擁有豐富而美麗的紋飾。

可以看見在圍兜的頸項處，以成串的回字紋圍成一整圈，圍兜面上則飾以如意雲紋、蝴蝶，中間並有雷紋的變化。在頸項上，有美麗的琉璃扣作為裝飾。

Square Bibs (1)

This square bib (Figure 76) is from northern China. Around the collar of the bib is a meander pattern. On the bib are embroideries of *ru-yi* clouds, butterfly motifs, and thunder patterns. Around the collar are also beautiful decorative buttons. All the motifs were embroidered using refined chain stitches.

方形の面白さその1

#76は、中国北方の作品で、四角い形をしています。この涎掛けはチェーン．ステッチという特殊な刺繍法で、色とりどりの美しい文様が飾られています。首周りには回字紋が一回り並んでおり、さらに如意雲、蝶などがあり、綺麗な瑠璃のボタンも付けられています。

Fig · #76

• 123 •

Fig.#77

⑦ 方形的趣味之二

#77也是方形的圍兜。作者以
十字繡的手法，在圍兜面上繡
出一隻隻美麗的鳳鳥，表現出
吉祥如意的祈福意味。

Square Bibs (2)

Figure 77 is also a square bib. The
cross-stitch method is used to
embroider gorgeous phoenixes
that express the well wishes of
the person who made the bib.

方形の面白さその2

#77では、クロスステッチという技
法で綺麗な鳳凰が何羽も描かれた。
めでたい雰囲気溢れる文様です。

第肆章

有趣的圍兜 Chapter 4 Bibs of Interest
第四章 面白い涎掛け

(78)

背心式的圍兜之一

這只圍兜有點類似背心，但其前後兩片為分開式的設計，所以仍然屬於圍兜。＃78全件由十分華麗的絲緞布料製成，面上織有象徵權力與富貴的團龍紋飾布紋，判斷很有可能是宮裡的用品。以龍的紋飾來說，明朝以前，龍的拇指多是分開的，清晰可辨；清朝以後才出現輪狀的五爪龍，也因此，這件圍兜可能是清朝時期的作品。

這只圍兜除了材質高貴，並以華麗的盤長織帶為滾邊裝飾，相當富麗堂皇。

The Vest-style Bib (1)

This bib (Figure 78) looks like a vest, but because the front and back panels are separated, it is still considered a bib. The design of this bib is extremely powerful, as there are embroideries of the mighty dragon on it. Because of its exquisite embroidery technique and use of high quality fabric, it was very likely used in the palace. Dragons, before and during the Ming Dynasty, were rendered with separate thumbs, and it was only in the Qing Dynasty that they were drawn with five wheel-like claws. Therefore, this bib is most likely from the Qin Dynasty.

ベスト風の涎掛け

#78はベストに見えますが、前後が分かれているため、やはり涎掛けであります。龍の文様といえば14世紀から16世紀にかける明の時代の龍は、爪がそれぞれ分かれており、一本一本はっきりと見て取れます。その後の清の時代に、初めて車輪状の5つ爪龍が現れました。したがってこの涎掛けは清の時代ものと判断してよいでしょう。非常に華麗なシルク地を使っており、権力と富貴を象徴する龍の文様が布を織る段階で織り込まれています。上等な生地を使っているほか、盤長結び文様の帯で縁取りをしているので、とても高級感がするものです。皇太子が使ったものかもしれません。

Fig・#78

背心式的圍兜之二

＃79這只圍兜也是類似背心式的設計，在絲質的面上，以紅、綠分為上下兩部份，並繡有豐富的圖案紋飾，相當具有童趣。這裡可以見到貓與蝶、梅花鹿，酷似花園一景，相當地生活化。可以想像縫製這只圍兜的母親，把花園中常見的景致一一繡入圍兜中，滿心歡喜地與孩兒分享人世間的美景。而在圍兜的邊上，繡有回紋裝飾。整體來說，這只圍兜也是治華麗與童趣於一爐的類型。

The Vest-style Bib (2)

Figure 79 is also a vest-style bib, separated into the top and bottom halves by red and green silk. Here, we see embroidery of cats, butterflies, deer, and an entire garden filled with flowers and leaves. The whole piece is lively and playful, and one can imagine that the mother who made this wanted to stitch the life of a garden right into her baby's bib.

ベスト風の涎掛け —その2

＃79もベスト風のデザインで、シルクの生地で赤と緑が上下に分かれ、

賑やかで可愛らしい文様が施されています。まるで庭園の一角にいるようで、花や、猫、蝶、鹿などがいます。庭園で見てきた様々な動物を、子供と分かち合うために、母親はこの涎掛けに縫い込んだでしょう。周りの縁に回字紋の飾りがあり、全体的には華やかさと可愛らしさを併せ持っています。

第参部 造型特殊的圍兜

Fig・#79

(80) 特殊的圍兜之一

＃80是相當特殊的作品，把圍兜、肚兜與圍裙一口氣設計在一起。整件作品以上半部的小方形與下半部的大方型上下相連組成，穿上它，可以一次罩住小孩的前胸與腹部，一點也不怕小娃兒弄髒了身體，下方的布可以當作肚兜，也可以當成圍裙使用。

這件罕見的圍兜加肚兜，是黎平一帶少數民族的作品。面上有非常豐富的幾何紋飾，包括鳥紋、卍字紋等，圍兜部分的圖飾則排成一個深V字型，精細的程度一點也不輸給漢人的作品。

Special Bibs (1)

Figure 80 is a very uniquely designed bib—it combines the bib with the undergarment and apron. The small rectangle on the top and the larger rectangle on the bottom sufficiently cover the baby's entire body so that it doesn't have any chance of getting dirty.

This rare bib-undergarment-apron combo piece is from a minority tribe in Liping. The stitching includes the swastika and bird motifs.

特殊な涎掛けその1

#80は相当特殊なもので、涎掛け、腹掛け、前掛けを併せたような形です。子供に着せると、前胸とお腹がすっぽり覆われ、服を汚す心配が全くありません。

これは黎平辺りの少数民族の作品で、びっしりと鳥、「萬」字などの幾何学紋が刺繍されていて、胸元のところには文様がV字型に並べられています。全体の出来具合は、漢民族の作品に少しも見劣りしません。

Fig . #80

81

特殊的圍兜之二

#81是一件少數民族的作品，有點像盔甲的造型，相當特殊與罕見。#81在圍兜頸項處是相當柔美的花瓣造型，面上也繡有紅、紫、粉紅相間的花卉；但在圍兜下方則風格一變，銀製的圓形突出裝飾，圍著一隻張開雙翅的蝴蝶，乍看之下，有點像古時戰士使用的盔甲，平添一股威武之氣，也與上方的柔美形成一剛、一柔的強烈對比。

Special Bibs (2)

Figure 81 is another bib from a minority tribe in Yunnan. It looks almost like armor, which is very unique. Around the collar are soft, feminine floral designs of reds, purples, and pinks. In contrast, the bottom part of the bib has a very different feel to it—the silver discs look like a suit of armor, giving it a masculine, aggressive sense. The contrast between the top half of the bib and the bottom half makes this piece especially dynamic.

特殊な涎掛けその2

#81も少数民族によるもので、鎧に似ていて、大変珍しいものです。首周りには赤、紫、桃色など綺麗な花によって柔和な雰囲気を出していますが、下の方では雰囲気ががらりと変わります。金属で作られた丸い突起の配列が一羽の蝶を囲んで、まるで古代の戦士が付けていた鎧のように猛猛しい感じが加えられ、上の方と強い対比になっています。

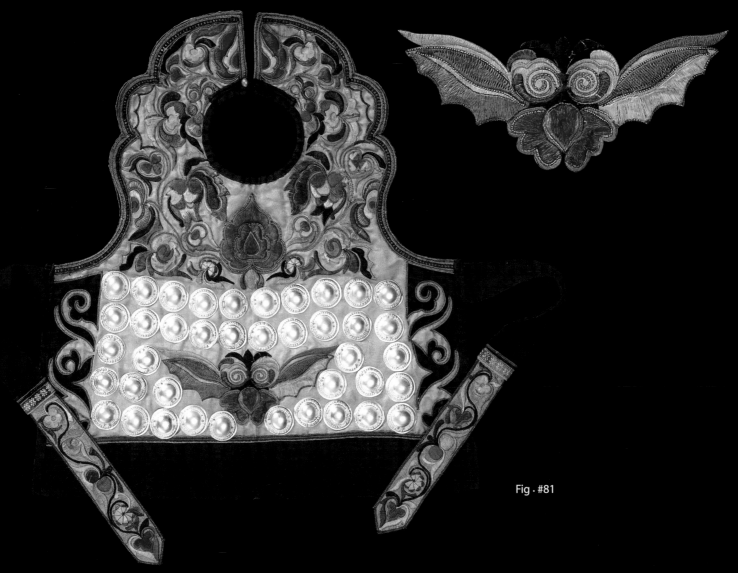

Fig . #81

Fig.・#82

⑧⑵

特殊的圍兜之三

#82這只圍兜是收藏自雲南一帶的作品。藍紫色的布面上，佈滿了如意雲紋的各種變化，看起來十分豐富典雅，也是以單一主題進行變化的成功之作。

Special Bibs (3)

Figure 82 was collected from the Yunnan region. The *ru-yi* patterns embroidered on the blue background make it very elegant and understated.

特殊な涎掛けその3

#82は雲南辺りから収集した作品で、紫がかった青い生地に、様々な形に変化した如意雲紋が広がっています。雅やかな雰囲気を漂わせるこの涎掛けは、如意雲のような単一の主題に、様々な変化を持たせた成功例と言えましょう。

第 ④ 部　美麗的驚歎號—霞帔

Part IV --- **Beautiful Exclamation – Capelets**

第四部 --- 美しすぎるほどの肩掛け

造型之美  Chapter 1　The Beauty of Design

第一章　造形の美

（83）

柳葉霞帔

#83的霞帔，美的令人讚嘆。八片柳葉狀的葉片，每一葉片滾著極細緻的滾邊，彷彿畫框一樣，將葉片面上美麗的一幅幅畫，襯托得更脫俗精彩，八個葉片，就是八幅精緻的宮廷畫。

這只收集自浙江紹興一帶的霞帔，值得仔細品味欣賞，仔細看，霞帔面上繡了喜鵲登梅，代表喜上眉梢；有蓮花蓮藕，代表出淤泥而不染；有石榴，象徵多子；還有一個翹著腿，睜大了眼睛的吹簫女子，顯得十分俏皮。除了葉片的滾邊，讓這些刺繡看來更加出色，創作者選用的紅、藍、粉紅等色澤，也流露清新討喜的氣質，讓人回味再三。

Elaborate Capelet

The beauty of this capelet (Figure 83) is extraordinary. The eight leaf-like petals of the capelet are all framed with rolled edges, making each leaf like a framed painting in a palace.

This piece is collected from Zhejiang Shaoxin region. Look at the details—there is a pair of magpies, which represent happiness and love; lotus flowers, which represent purity; and pomegranates, which represent many children and grandchildren. There's even a young, wide-eyed girl with one leg kicked up, playing the flute.

柳葉形の肩掛け

#83の肩掛けは、ため息が出るほど見事な出来映えです。周りに満遍なく縁取りがなされ、額縁のように中の絵を囲み、その美しさを一層引き出しています。八枚の柳葉は、まるで八枚の細緻な宮廷絵画のように見えます。

浙江紹興辺りから収集したこの肩掛けは、じっくり楽しめる傑作です。よく見ると、「カササギと梅」、「蓮の花と蓮根」（汚泥の中でも染まらずにいられるという意味）などのめでたい組み合わせがあるほか、石榴という「子孫繁栄」を意味する文様もあります。さらに、笛を吹いている活発そうな少女がいます。この作品は、縁取りの手法が大変上手いばかりでなく、赤、青、桃色の色の選択も上手で、爽やかで愛らしい感じが伝わってきます。

Fig · #83

(84) 蝶形霞帔

好一隻別緻的蝴蝶！＃84是
北京一帶的霞帔作品，整件
霞帔就是一隻美麗的蝴蝶，
穿戴在孩兒身上更顯得出
眾，讓人不忍轉開視線。

創作這只霞帔的婦女，在霞
帔邊上勾勒出彩蝶翩翩起舞
的美麗身形，蝶形葉片垂墜
在孩兒胸前，顯得相當特
別，另外作者運用了不同色
澤的挖雲與貼布手法，妝點
出彩蝶身上的斑點，藍、橘
的強烈對比，耀眼而出色。
在霞帔的頸項處，另有金屬
的雙喜扣，使這件美麗的霞
帔增添了幾許華貴之美。

Butterfly Capelet

This butterfly capelet (Figure
84) comes from Beijing. It is
almost costume-like, with all
the details of a butterfly about
to take flight. The contrast of
blue and orange is especially
eye- catching. And notice
the gold button at the neck,
which makes this capelet
even more exquisite.

Fig . #84

蝶形の肩掛け

なんと奇抜なデザインなのでしょう！

この肩掛けは北京から収集した作品で、全体が蝶の形をしていて、実際に子供に着せたら一層人の
目を惹くことでしょう。美しく舞う蝶の姿に形作っており、蝶の羽根がちょうど胸元に垂れ下がっ
てくるという計算はほんとうに心憎いものです。さらにオープン．ワーク．エンブロイダリーと
アップリケの技法により、青、橙色などの対比色で蝶の羽根の美しい斑点を見事に作りあげまし
た。首周りには金屬のボタンが付けられており、一層高級感を漂わせています。

桃形霞帔

八個桃子連在一起，中間還有八角的星形裝飾，#85的霞帔充分展現了圖形變化的趣味與美感，淡淡的嫩綠色，夾雜在粉紅與嫩黃之間，予人春天清新無邪的喜悦感受。霞帔面上，繡有多種花卉圖形，是裝飾性很強的一件霞帔。

Peach Capelet

Eight peach-shaped petals are connected to an eight-pointed star in the middle. The light grass-green edges and the use of lavenders and powdery pinks make this piece full of innocence and naiveté. (Figure 85)

桃形の肩掛け

8つの桃が肩を寄せ合い、真ん中に八角形の星が飾られていて、#85は図形の変化に富む面白い一点です。配色の気配りも見どころで、淡い緑が桃色と薄黄色の間に入れられ、春の初々しさを演出しています。また様々な花が飾られ、賑やかでうきうきするものです。

#85

86

霞帔之美之一

＃86這只霞帔是收集自湖南一帶的作品，整體設計顯得相當精緻典雅。首先，環繞著頸項處的是一圈華美的緞帶高領，上面有一個接一個的盤長紋飾與萬福（卍）紋；霞帔面上則以別緻的如意雲紋進行鏤空的變化；下接長長的流蘇予以點綴。

在色澤的搭配上，這件霞帔也有獨到之處，嫩綠的色彩配上鮮橘色，加上高領緞帶上的點點粉紅，感覺十分典雅而高貴。

The Beauty of the Capelet (1)

This piece comes from Hunan (Figure 86). The design of this piece is very intricate and elegant. First, the high collar is made from silk ribbon, embroidered with swastikas. On the capelet are ru-yi cloud motifs that look as though they are moving upwards through the sky. The final touch is the addition of the luscious orange tassels on the bottom. In its color combinations—pale green with bright orange—this capelet is also very sophisticated.

Fig · #86

美しい肩掛けその1

＃86は湖南辺りから収集した作品で、精緻かつ典雅な一点です。首周りのところに盤長結びと萬字紋が帯状に刺繍されています。その下に如意雲紋が透かし彫りの技法で施され、そして一番下には長い房飾りがぶら下がっています。配色に至っても、優れた工夫が見られ、柔らかい緑色と鮮やかな黄色、それに首周りの桃色との組み合わせは、優雅で上品な感じが漂います。

(87)

霞帔之美之二

＃87是一件精緻又豐富多彩的霞帔。縫製這只霞帔的婦女，顯然花了相當細密的心思，才創造出這樣豐富的霞被之美來。

首先，這只霞帔採用了花瓣造型的葉片，霞帔展開時，就像一朵盛開的花朵，而在八個花瓣之上，則使用特殊的染布繡技巧，創造出極具漸層感、深淺不一的特殊效果，另外還繡上豐富的花鳥動物紋飾，包括：松鼠、葡萄、老虎、梅花鹿、雙鳥、魚戲蓮與貓蝶（耄耋）等等。造型之美，令人目不暇給。

這件霞帔在頸項處，繡以「富貴吉祥」四字，希望為孩兒帶來好運，長長的流蘇則以紅、綠兩色混搭，是整體看來非常豐富的一件作品。

The Beauty of the Capelet (2)

This capelet (Figure 87) is both intricate and colorful. It is clear that the woman who made it put a lot of thought into its design.

First, the capelet is made up of flower-like petals. When the capelet is spread out, it looks like a blooming flower. On each petal, a special dyeing technique is used that gives the color of the fabric a non-uniform wash. In addition, every petal is embroidered with intricately detailed flowers, birds, and various animals, including a squirrel, a tiger, a deer, and pairs of birds, fish, and cats. It is really quite remarkable how much detail is in this capelet.

At the collar, the characters for "wealth and peace" are embroidered, wishing good fortune to the child who wears this capelet. The long red and green tassels give this piece yet another dimension.

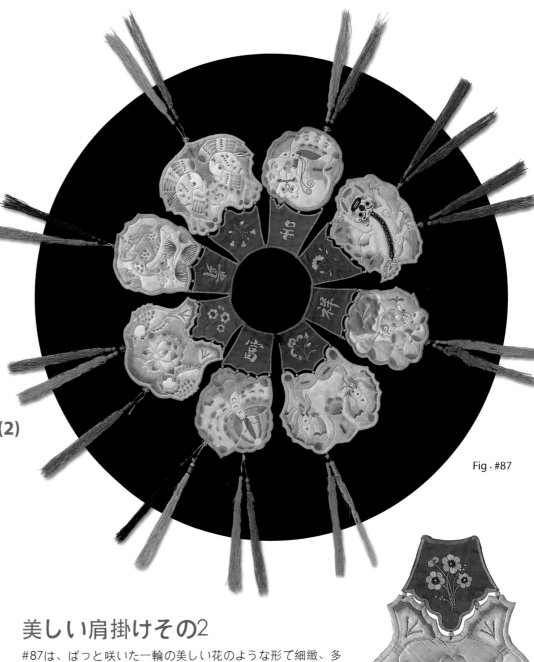

Fig · #87

美しい肩掛けその2

#87は、ぱっと咲いた一輪の美しい花のような形で細緻、多彩を極め、大変手間暇掛かった傑作と言えましょう。染色と刺繍の両方の技法が採られ、素晴らしい濃淡を出しているため、花々が生き生きとして見えます。ほかにリス、葡萄、虎、鹿、鳥、魚と蓮の花の組み合わせと、猫と蝶の組み合わせなど、目が迷ってしまうほどの、様々なめでたい文様が色鮮やかに描かれています。首周りの「吉祥富貴」という字は、文字通り子供に幸せを祈る縁起のいい言葉です。

霞帔之美之三

＃88這只霞帔採用了多種刺繡技巧，展現出豐富完整的刺繡之美。這只霞帔設計成四個葉片，邊上散佈了二十個壽桃形狀的流蘇綴飾，這些桃子形狀的流蘇都採用貼布技法製作而成，並使用粉紅、紅、黃、綠等不同顏色，相當特別；和一般慣用的長形流蘇相比，又展露出相當不同的風情，可愛中摻雜著幾許天真與俏皮。

霞帔面上，創作者使用了精細的破絲繡，繡出多枚圓圓的團壽紋飾，並以皮金技巧來裝飾；邊上另繡上吉祥的如意雲紋，採用盤銀的手法加以點綴。

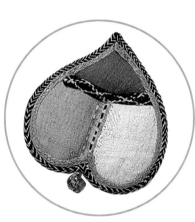

The Beauty of the Capelet (3)

This capelet (Figure 88) employs many different types of embroidery techniques and showcases the beauty of embroidery in general. This piece is separated into four different panels. Around the circumference are twenty peach-shaped attachments that act like tassels. Compared to traditional tassels, these peaches express a different kind of style of design—one that is more playful and adorable.

美しい肩掛けその3

四枚の生地の下に、さらに5つずつの桃が房飾りとして付けられ、見事な形をする肩掛けです。桃は全てアップリケによるもので、桃色、赤、黄色、緑などの明るい色が使われ、房飾りとしては、天真爛漫な感じがする珍しいデザインだと言えましょう。四枚の本体には、スプリット．シルク．ステッチという精緻な刺繡技法が取り入れられ、「寿」の字を丸くした文樣が並んでいます。如意雲紋はその外回りの縁にあり、両方の文樣とも光る金か銀の糸で仕上げいるので、大変贅沢感が漂うものです。

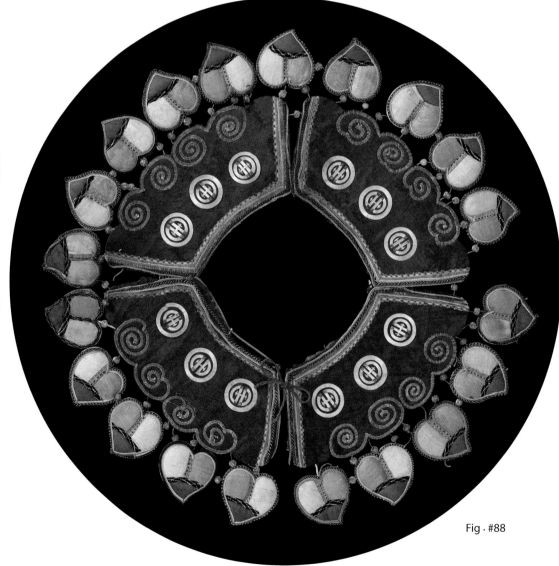

Fig．#88

成人霞帔之一

#89是一件非常美麗的霞帔,完整性非常高,以其尺寸大小來看,應該是屬於成人使用的霞帔,一併收納進本書,可以和孩童的霞帔比對並作欣賞。

這只霞帔設計成三層的柳葉葉片,以翠綠、紅、白三色為主色調的葉片層層相疊,非常美麗。柳葉面的刺繡也相當精彩,可以看到有花卉、太湖石、人物玩耍、人拿扇、漁舟、魚、蟹之類樓台水榭的文人雅好,另外也有象徵吉祥之意的「暗八仙」。這件美麗的霞帔,無論是柳葉造型或面上的刺繡,都表現的相當出色,值得細細品味欣賞。

Capelets for Adults (1)

This is a gorgeous capelet that, judging by its dimensions, was probably worn by an adult. It is interesting to compare this capelet with the capelets for children that this book showcases.

This piece (Figure 89) is made of three layers of leaf-shaped petals. Each layer is represented by a certain color—green on the top, red in the middle, and white on the bottom. On each leaf there is embroidery of very detailed images—you can see flowers, rocks, figures playing, figures holding fans, fishing boats, fish, and crabs. The intricacy in the design of this capelet is truly astounding.

大人の肩掛けその1

#89はまさに非の打ち所の無い一点です。大きさから見ると大人用と思われるので、子供用のものと見比べて頂こうと、あえて本書に取り入れた作品です。

形としては、柳の葉っぱを並べたような生地が3重構造になっていて、色はそれぞれ緑、赤、白が主です。形のほか、刺繡の飾りも見事なもので、花、太湖石、戯れている人、扇子を手にする人、漁舟、魚、蟹など文人好みの文様がたっぷりと飾られています。この美しい肩掛けは、柳葉の三重構造にしろ、刺繡の出来具合にしろ、いずれも大変見事としか言いようがありません。

Fig・#89

成人霞帔之二

　#90是收集自山東一帶的霞帔，以尺寸來看，也是屬於成人所使用。這件霞帔被設計成直式的四個層次，從上到下，包括長型葉片、如意雲紋、柳葉葉片與長形流蘇，形式相當特殊。

　第三層的柳葉葉片是視覺上的重點，柳葉面上，繡有精緻的刺繡紋飾，包括有花卉、鳥、金魚、石榴、蝴蝶等，相當豐富而美麗。在流蘇部分，設計成粉紅、綠、紫三種顏色，用色極為奔放而突出。

Capelets for Adults (2)

This piece (Figure 90) is from Shandong region and, judging by its dimensions, was also likely worn by an adult. There are four layers to this capelet, including narrow leaf-shaped petals, *ru-yi* clouds, and long tassels.

The third layer of leaves is the main focus, with its beautiful embroidery of flowers, birds, goldfish, pomegranates, and butterflies. The designs and color combinations are absolutely gorgeous.

大人の肩掛けその2

　#90は、山東辺りから収集したもので、大きさから見ると、やはり大人用のものと思われます。上から下まで、細長い葉状のもの、如意雲のもの、柳葉のもの、長い房飾りと、4重構造になっていて、大変珍しいものです。

　見どころは第3重の柳葉で、花、鳥、金魚、石榴、蝶など、精緻な刺繍が施されています。房飾りは桃色、緑、紫で、色使いが大変大胆で他の作品と比べても抜きん出ているすばらしい作品だと思います。

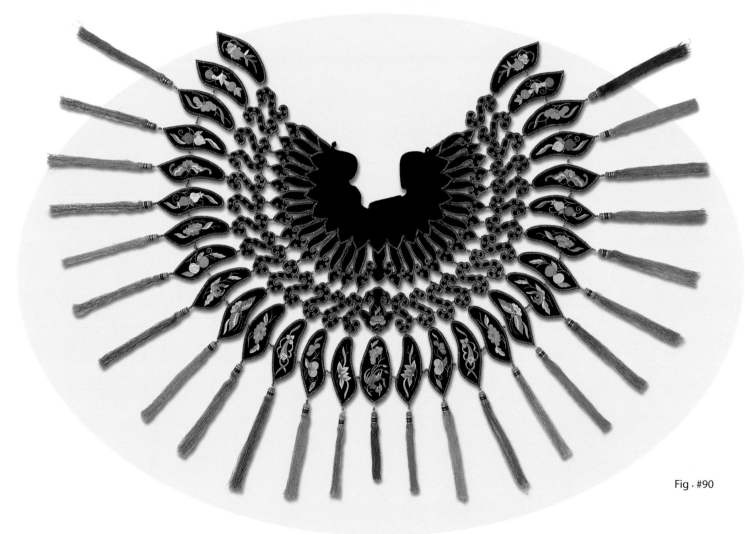

Fig．#90

91

成人霞帔之三

#91這只霞帔的剪裁十分具有立體感，設計為八個葉片，霞帔面上繡有許多吉祥的圖飾，如萬字紋、方勝、星星、白菜等，並有「富貴雙全」、「福祿滿堂」的字樣。霞帔在胸前設計有紅色的長穗，另在葉片下方刻意剪裁成一個個如意雲紋，雲紋下方再綴以色彩斑斕的穗子，整體設計顯得十分別出心裁。

Capelets for Adults (3)

This capelet (Figure 91) is composed of eight leaflets. Auspicious motifs such as the swastika, the lozenge, and stars are embroidered. Auspicious characters are also included. The long red tassels make this an outstanding capelet.

Fig · #91

大人の肩掛けその3

#91の肩掛けは、裁断により形に立体感を持たせています。8枚からなる本体の上に、「萬」字紋、星、白菜(清らかなイメージ)など、沢山の縁起物が飾られています。下のほうには、「富貴双全」、「福祿満堂」、つまり、「財運、出世運に恵まれる」という意味の言葉が書かれています。胸元には赤く長い房飾りがあり、また8枚の本体の下の縁を如意雲紋の形にし、その下にさらに色とりどりの房飾りを付けました。ほかの肩掛けにはない工夫が強く印象に残る一点です。

參考書目 / **Bibliography**

1. 中國傳統吉祥圖案　　　　　　　　李祖庭主編　　　　　　上海科學普及出版社

2. 吉祥如意　　　　　　　　　　　　黃永松總策劃　　　　　　漢聲雜誌

3. 國吉祥圖像大觀　　　　　　　　　左漢中編著　　　　　　　湖南美術出版社

4. 中國吉祥圖案　　　　　　　　　　李蒼彦編　　　　　　　　台北南天書局有限公司

5. 中國傳統吉祥寓意圖案　　　　　　天津楊柳青畫社

6. 吉祥百圖　　　　　　　　　　　　黃永松總策劃　　　　　　漢聲雜誌

7. 山東剪紙民俗　　　　　　　　　　山曼編著　　　　　　　　濟南山版社

8. 台灣民間文化藝術　　　　　　　　李莎莉主編　　　　　　　（財）福祿文教基金會
　　　　　　　　　　　　　　　　　　　　　　　　　　　　南天書局有限公司

9. 清代台灣民間刺繡　　　　　　　　黏碧華/陳達明　　　　　苗栗縣立文化中心

10. 刺繡針法百種　　　　　　　　　　黏碧華　　　　　　　　　雄師美術

11. 母親的花朵兒　　　　　　　　　　王寧宇/楊庚緒　　　　　三秦出版社

12. 吉祥童帽　Stories of Chinese Children's Hats　　藍采如　　　　　麗嬰房股份有限公司

13. 情繫揹兒帶　Bonding via Baby Carriers　　藍劉玉嬌/藍采如/林柏薇　麗嬰房股份有限公司

14. Outlines of Chinese Symbolism and Art Motives　　Williams　　　　Dovers

藍采如 **Christi Lan Lin**

■ 藍 采如 **Christi Lan Lin**

台大理學士，美國北科大生物科學碩士
麗嬰房副總經理—1997年退休
台北故宮博物院志工12年
曾著有「吉祥童帽」、「情繫揹兒帶」

Christi received her MA in biological science from Northern Colorado University.
She has been working at Les Enphants Co. as Vice President until she retired in 1997.
Christi has been a volunteer docent at National Palace Museum in Taipei for more than 12 years.
She is the author of *Stories of Chinese Children's Hats: Symbolism and Folklore*
and *Bonding Via Baby Carriers: The Art and Soul Of The Miao and Dong People*.

台湾大学理学士、アメリカコロラド大学生物学修士
麗嬰房(株)副社長にて1997年退職
台湾台北故宮博物館ボランテイアガイドにて12年
「吉祥童帽」「情繁背児帯」など著書あり

藍劉玉嬌 **Yu-Chiao Liu**

■ 藍 劉玉嬌 **Yu-Chiao Liu Lan** （日本語翻訳）

日本東京女醫專畢—眼科醫生・行醫42年後退休
曾與女兒藍采如、外孫女林柏薇合著並翻譯「情繫揹兒帶」

Dr. Liu received her MD degree from Tokyo Women's Medical College in 1940.
She practiced as an ophthalmologist until her retirement in the 1980s.
She is the co-author and translator in *Bonding Via Baby Carriers: The Art And Soul Of The Miao and Dong People*.

日本東京女子医専卒——眼科医
眼科医として活躍42年、リタイヤ中
女児 藍 采如、孫 林 柏薇との合作で「情繁背児帯」の創作と翻訳

林柏薇 **brenda Lin**

■ 林 柏薇 **brenda Lin** （英語翻訳）

美國哥倫比亞大學文學創作碩士
曾著有 "Wealth Ribbon - Taiwan Bound, America Bound"
並與外婆藍劉玉嬌、母親藍采如合著及翻譯「情繫揹兒帶」
現為自由作家

brenda received her MFA from Columbia University in Creative Writing.
She is the author of *Wealth Ribbon: Taiwan Bound, America Bound*.
She is also the co-author and the translator of *Bonding Via Baby Carriers: The Art and Soul Of The Miao And Dong People*

アメリカコロンビア大学文学創作学修士
「Wealth Ribbon」-(アメリカ版)の作者
その他 祖母 藍 劉玉嬌、母 藍 采如との合作で創作及び翻訳「情繁背児帯」あり
現在はフリーライター

濃 情 滿 襟

Symbolism of Chinese Children's Bibs: A Mother's Affectionate Embrace
胸いっぱいの幸せ

發 行 人	林泰生	Publisher	Eric Lin
作 者	藍采如	Author	Christi Lan Lin
日文翻譯	藍劉玉嬌	Translator (Japanese)	Yu-Chiao Liu Lan
英文翻譯	林柏薇	Translator (English)	brenda Lin
收 藏 者	藍采如	Collector	Christi Lan Lin
總 策 劃	藍采如	Executive Planner	Christi Lan Lin
主 編	蘭 薰	Editor	Nicole Lan
攝 影	高宗義	Photographer	Zong-Yi Gao
設 計	陳潤淇	Art Designer	Mary Chen

出版發行　麗嬰房股份有限公司

地　址　中華民國台北市114內湖區陽光街321巷60號

電　話　886-2-8797-6699

傳　真　886-2-8797-5577

印　刷　秋雨印刷股份有限公司

初版一刷　西元2006年3月

定　價　新台幣780元

客服專線・購買專線　0800-000-618

網路訂購・インターネット購買　www.phland.com

Publisher　Les Enphants Co.

No.60, Lane 321, Yang-kwang Street

Taipei, Taiwan, R.O.C.

TEL: 886-2-8797-6699

FAX: 886-2-8797-5577

Printer　Choice Color Printing Co.

Published in 2006 by Les Enphants Co.

Price　US$ 39.95

International book order contact:

Phylis Lan Lin, Executive Director
University of Indianapolis Press
1400 E. Hanna Ave.
Indianapolis, Indiana 46227
lin@uindy.edu
http://www.uindy.edu//universitypress